Memo to a
College Trustee

Memo to a College Trustee

A Report on Financial and Structural Problems of the Liberal College

by **Beardsley Ruml**

Part 4: Achievement of the Possible
by **Donald H. Morrison**

Prepared for and Transmitted by
The Fund for the Advancement of Education

McGRAW-HILL BOOK COMPANY, INC.
New York   Toronto   London

MEMO TO A COLLEGE TRUSTEE

First Edition

PREFACE

This Report is concerned with a cluster of crucial questions: How can the American liberal colleges meet their responsibilities with respect to the fostering of liberal education? How can they serve their important purpose in helping to prepare the next generation of adults to deal wisely and humanely with the problems and opportunities of an increasingly complex world? How can they make the contribution to teaching and to scholarship that is required?

More specifically, how can our colleges—and our universities, too—organize their faculties, their teaching programs, their facilities and their finances to provide liberal education for twice as many students as today, a liberal education of constantly improving quality?

Today these institutions of higher learning are not organized to meet this challenge. They will be able to do so only if they receive greatly increased support and understanding from without and undergo substantial improvements from within. This Report deals with possible internal improvements. It is transmitted as a *Memo to a College Trustee* because the trustees of the colleges have final responsibility and authority for the performance of their institutions. Accordingly, they must understand the issues that the liberal college faces and find solutions within the specific structure of the college for which they are responsible. It is hoped, however, that college presidents, faculty members and others who also carry heavy responsibility for the future of the colleges will find this document useful.

The liberal colleges today are squeezed between limited financial resources and the necessity of substantial increases in faculty salaries. They must find a solution to this situation if they are to maintain their quality while they meet the increasing demands that face them. For a considerable number of these colleges the issue may not be merely whether they can hold their quality but whether they can even survive.

It has been a major purpose of the Fund for the Advancement of Education ever since its establishment by the Ford Foundation in 1951 to provide support to imaginative colleges, to their administrators and to faculty members in both public and private institutions of higher learning. It is gratifying to observe the accelerated efforts that are being made in many institutions to improve the practices and the quality of higher education. Yet the problems are rushing at the colleges so fast that only with the most vigorous efforts will they be able even to hold their present position.

In the search for ideas which might be useful to the colleges, it was natural for the Fund officials to turn once again to Beardsley Ruml, whose name has become synonymous with creative thinking about stubborn social problems. Several years ago, Mr. Ruml prepared a report to the Fund entitled *Teaching Salaries Then and Now*. The publication of this report helped highlight the need to correct the serious erosion in teachers' salaries which had occurred over half a century. Mr. Ruml is best known to the public as the inventor of the 1943 national "pay-as-you-go" plan of income tax collection. He was at one time Chairman of the Board of the Federal Reserve Bank of New York and Chairman of the Board of R. H. Macy & Company. He has made important contributions to the Committee for Economic Development and the National Planning Association. But Mr. Ruml's experience extends well beyond finance and business. He earned his Ph.D. in Psychology and Education at the University of

Chicago. He was for some years Dean of Social Sciences and Professor of Education at the University of Chicago. As Director of the Laura Spelman Rockefeller Memorial from 1923–1929 he worked extensively with colleges and universities; and he has maintained an active interest in higher education over many years.

Last year the Fund asked Mr. Ruml to examine the financial and structural aspects of liberal colleges as they affect and are affected by the curriculum and teaching program of such colleges.

Since these matters are intimately related to the internal "system of government" by which decisions are made, programs formed and resources allocated within a college, the Fund asked Donald Morrison* to supplement Mr. Ruml's inquiry with an analysis of the internal workings of the liberal college. Donald Morrison received his Ph.D. in Political Science at Princeton University. He has been an Assistant Professor of Political Science at Louisiana State University, Administrative Aide to the Bureau of the Budget of the Federal government, and later Professor of Government at Dartmouth College. He has been Chairman of the Committee on Utilization of College Teaching Resources of the Fund for the Advancement of Education and has made a report to the Carnegie Corporation on administrative problems of higher education.

Mr. Ruml and Mr. Morrison are, respectively, a Trustee and the Provost of Dartmouth College. Each has drawn, however, on information and experience from a variety of institutions and situations, extending beyond the particular institution with which he is now associated. Each has written in his personal capacity and, of course, their associates—the Trustees, Administrative Officers and Faculty at Dartmouth—are not responsible for, nor identified with, the findings and statements of the separate authors.

The first draft of the Report as received from the authors was submitted by the Fund to 100 distinguished college and university presidents, faculty members, Trustees and other well-qualified observers in the belief that their reactions would be useful to the authors in preparing the final draft. To these busy and able people the Fund is profoundly grateful. Their reactions were prompt and vigorous. As one might expect with a document as provocative as this, the critics varied widely in their comments, but virtually all agreed that it was a stimulating and important document which should be published promptly and given wide distribution.

The comments which were received were extremely helpful, and the Report as it is here presented is the result of substantial revision, in eliminating important ambiguities and in expanding sections that were too brief to be meaningful.

The Report is being published exactly as it was finally submitted to the Fund by the authors. It is in no sense a statement of Fund policy. But it is testimony of the Fund's conviction that fresh ideas and vigorous discussion are essential ingredients of progress in American education.

The Board and staff of the Fund for the Advancement of Education express their deep appreciation to Mr. Ruml and to Mr. Morrison for the great personal expenditure of time and thought they have invested in the preparation of this analysis and Report.

CLARENCE H. FAUST, PRESIDENT

The Fund for the Advancement of Education

On March 17, 1959, after this Report had gone to the printer, Donald Morrison passed away very suddenly. Through his creativity, skill and devotion he had made a lasting contribution to American higher education, far beyond the institutions he served and all out of proportion to his relatively brief academic career. The Fund's staff, which had benefited greatly from his wise counsel and friendship, joins the academic community in expressing a deep sense of loss for this talented and humane man.

CONTENTS

FOREWORD

This Report is directed to the financial and structural problems of the traditional, independent 4-year liberal college. At the same time much that is said here applies to the liberal-college component in the broad sweep of the private or public university. However, the university taken as a whole, with its specialized graduate and research activities, its libraries, laboratories and museums, its several professional schools, and its commitment to extension courses and adult education, has purposes not shared directly by most liberal colleges. To these university purposes, considerations bearing specifically on the liberal college do not necessarily apply.

The economic and financial problems of the liberal college, together with the structural setting in which they exist, are so central to the life and character of the college that they deeply influence its entire educational purpose and program. This is particularly true as they affect the curriculum and methods of instruction.

It would have been possible to proceed from the point of view that the economic and financial needs of the college arise from a duty to protect a curriculum and methods of instruction of unquestioned merit and revealed value. On the other hand, it is possible to recognize that present economic and financial problems have arisen to an important degree because developments within the control of the college have weakened its ability to carry on its central educational purposes. To the extent that this is so, the true present economic and financial needs from external sources of the liberal college cannot be convincingly estimated. This second point of view is taken in this Report.

More particularly, we are concerned with a number of economic, financial and structural issues that must be resolved if the liberal college is to have the strength and freedom to make its potential contribution to the best interests of liberal education.

The contribution of the liberal college to liberal education is of course made by the substance and quality of its program, and these matters are deliberately not discussed in this Report. There are so many different ways of creating a program that is good in substance, there is so much that can be properly said for and against both major and minor detail, that it seemed best to confine this Report to financial and structural problems. Here there is much to be discussed, and unless adequate financial and structural arrangements can be obtained, the essential purpose of the college cannot be realized.

This Report consists essentially of the observations, inferences and suggestions of its authors. It is not a "scientific" study, except in the sense that it is objective in spirit and is intended to contribute to an understanding of the liberal-college problem. Concrete illustrative material has been omitted because of the danger of presenting true but unfair and unrepresentative detail, vivid and suggestive though it might be. Other observers may well find statements in this Report inconsistent with their own experience, and inferences too sweeping to be justified by the obviously limited evidence that can be brought to this vast problem by any two persons. If so, they must rely on their own or different insights to come to their own or different conclusions. Or they may find that they can accept some, but not all, of the substance of this Report. Such differences are inevitable and welcome.

Discussion and criticism will certainly improve the knowledge that is needed to correct weaknesses that most observers will agree exist in the liberal-college system as it operates today.

Criticism of past and present practices and tendencies is not set forth for the purpose of indictment, nor to secure a conviction of guilt or error before a court of public opinion. Study of the present and how we managed to get where we are serves a useful purpose only if it suggests changes that promise to help us get where we would like to be. That the changes are drastic and urgently required is simply a result of a long period of erosion, a period during which nothing serious was apparently happening—save that the foundations and influence of the liberal college were being weakened, not by malice, but by neglect, by the hold of traditional thinking born of inertia and pride.

II

This Report on Financial and Structural Problems of the Liberal College is presented in five related parts.

Part 1, The Liberal College and Its Trustees, considers the liberal college as an instrument of liberal education, the authority and responsibilities of its Trustees, the suitability of the faculty as a body for jurisdiction over the design and administration of the curriculum, and finally suggests that the Trustees should find a different mechanism than the collective faculty to which responsibility for the curriculum should be assigned.

Part 2, Curriculum and Methods of Instruction, presents observations on the structure of the curriculum and the reasons for its great expansion over recent decades. Methods of instruction are examined, both as reflected in the weekly and yearly academic calendar and as they can be organized in a

variety of teaching units. The problem of building facilities
is mentioned as it relates to methods of instruction.

Part 3, Models of the Possible, is an arithmetical and theo-
retical analysis of what might be possible in terms of classes
of various sizes for the several methods of teaching, together
with tables of faculty compensation attainable under the assumptions on which the models were based. Models are presented for colleges of four different sizes, 800, 1,200, 1,800
and 3,000 students.

Part 4, Achievement of the Possible, discusses the practical situation arising from the attitudes of faculty members and administrative officers that must be recognized and
worked with if the liberal college, having accepted a model
in principle, is in the end to achieve it, at least in substantial
part.

Suggestions of alternative "mechanisms" to which the
college might look for initiative in making broad recommendations on the curriculum are presented, and their strengths
and inadequacies are discussed.

Part 5, The Informed Trustee, returns to the Trustee
as the locus of final responsibility and authority and considers
in some detail the information which he needs to perform
his function for the liberal college. The issues raised by academic freedom and tenure are noted, and the proper interest
of the Trustee is indicated. Finally, the necessity for an informed Trustee is again emphasized, if the Board of Trustees
is to fulfill its charter purposes, if it is to make the liberal
college the educational resource that this institution was designed to be.

Memo to a College Trustee

PART 1

The Liberal College
and Its Trustees

In recent years, an urgency and a new importance have been given to liberal education and, at the same time, a new and higher need has been seen for the liberal college. In this Report, concern for the liberal college results from a profound interest in liberal education. It is liberal education that discovers, defines and preserves the essential human values, that magnifies them through varieties of human association, real and imaginary, that protects them during struggles for economic and political power, that asserts the good, the beautiful and the true.

Interest in the liberal college is not in the institution on its own account. If liberal education could be better provided by eliminating the liberal college, it could be eliminated. As other means are found of promoting liberal education outside the jurisdiction of the liberal college, these means will be welcomed.

The liberal college may or may not be as important as free speech and the free press in all their forms as an instrument of value in promoting and protecting liberal education. Both the liberal college and the free press contribute to the liberal education of the people—but both are means to an end, not ends in themselves.

The liberal colleges are expected to formalize and suggest a variety of possible patterns that liberal education may properly take. Less often do we hear in high and responsible quarters dire predictions that the liberal college will be squeezed flat and will disappear between the pressure for curriculum enrichment at school levels junior to the college and the demand for a tougher and earlier vocationalism from business and from professional and technical institutions catering to the more mature. On the contrary, elementary and secondary schools are looking to the liberal college to define the essential substance of liberal education, to which they may conform or from which they may deviate as they please. And business and professional and higher technical establishments are calling on the liberal college to assure a breadth of educational preparation that will safeguard lifelong competence in the rapidly growing substance both of technical skill and of professional wisdom in practical fields.

The liberal college today finds itself, for the most part through no outstanding meritorious accomplishment of its own, the central hope for educational salvation. It is looked to for guidance in the selection of enterprises educationally worthy for the young, and, at the same time, for methods of preparing minds that will continue to be able to learn long after the formal processes of schooling of the individual have become things of the past.

Whether or not this new prestige of liberal education and the liberal college is a flight from an unsupportable present educational reality to the protection of a romantic unknown that seems responsive to a pressing need is interesting but of little practical importance. The practical problem today is to recognize this generally felt necessity, to improve the opportunities for liberal education, and to do what can be done to raise the performance of the liberal college so that it may meet in some fair measure what the evolving national welfare requires.

The widespread interest in the liberal college—evidenced not only by professional educators, but by alumni and students,

by statesmen and citizens generally, by fathers and mothers—
results in emphasis on a variety of related objectives, all of
which are properly assigned to the liberal college, and by
which in a variety of ways its performance is judged. It becomes necessary, therefore, to go to the root of the matter, to
inquire by what authority the liberal college derives its being
and its powers. On whom does final authority and responsibility rest? Can it be strengthened in respect to curriculum or
operation? By what means can purposeful change be insti-
tuted, and by what basic standards can a liberal college be
judged as having the potential for long-term usefulness?

Part 1 of the Report deals with these essential, if somewhat formal, considerations.

II

The liberal college is a corporate body holding powers,
privileges and immunities as charter rights granted by some
sovereign political authority. In a few cases, these charter
rights preceded the existence of the particular state that later
confirmed them. To the original charter rights there have
been added other rights pertaining to all corporate members
of the same class.

The existence of these charters is helpful in that they
specify what the institutions may do—and precisely who in
the institution is finally responsible for doing it. True, the
detail has been spelled out later by the chartered authorities
in bylaws and contracts, but the final locus of power is to be
found in the charter. The charter is the constitution for the
government of the college or university. It is from this point
we can best survey performance and appraise results in terms
of purpose.

Since the liberal college is a body corporate in the public
interest, the powers, privileges and immunities of its Trustees
are in fact duties and obligations. These rights are given by
the charter to the Trustees in order that they may be exer-

cised, and exercised by these particular persons or by their lawful successors. A single Trustee or the Trustees collectively may abdicate from their position of authority, but they cannot annul it; they may vacate their posts, but they cannot destroy them; they may delegate activities and decisions, but they cannot thereby avoid their own responsibilities.

The President of a liberal college is its chief executive officer and at the same time is the highest personal symbol of the college—to the public generally, and specifically to alumni and parents, to the officers and Trustees of other educational institutions, to legislative and other public bodies. Members of the faculty and of the student body, who naturally have more intimate associations within the institution than with the President himself, nevertheless look to him for suggestive leadership.

The carrying out of these executive and public activities is a delicate and time-consuming task, requiring qualities of efficient and perceptive understanding. But the true locus of the President's authority and responsibility lies elsewhere; it lies in his duty to organize the agenda for meetings of the Trustees and to take the initiative in bringing necessary information to their individual and collective attention. Most important of all in this is his leadership with respect to the educational program of the college. Suggestions as to what should be included on the agenda and what policies should be adopted may come from many sources, from individual Trustees or Committees of Trustees, from individual members of the faculty, from committees of the faculty, or from the faculty as a body, from alumni, from students, from parents, from articles in the lay and professional press. Regardless of source, the selection and the timing of subjects for the agenda is the President's job, and to this material he is expected to add his own personal interpretations and recommendations. It is the President's responsibility to carry out the decisions of the Trustees and to reflect in tangible and intangible ways the ambitions of the Trustees for the performance and service of the college.

The members of the faculty of a liberal college are the individuals through whom the teaching, writing and research of the college is principally carried on, although significant contributions in these fields not uncommonly come from the administrative staff, including, of course, the President. The members of the faculty are selected and retained because of professional competence in a wider or narrower field of knowledge, usually carrying or working toward a degree of doctor of philosophy, the conventional test of demonstrated competence in advanced and creative work in a designated subject matter.

The individual member of the faculty is given, subject to the operational requirements of his department, wide freedom of expression in his own classes, his own writing and in his professional speaking. It is common in most colleges that, at a certain time and after demonstrating intellectual and personal competence, he is given permanent tenure as well.

Due to an intolerable level of compensation, the long vacations and the conventional sabbatical year, though respected as ideals, have in fact, unfortunately, largely lost their function. They no longer serve as ways of keeping the members of the faculty alert, in close contact with their subjects and their colleagues, with time to think, to discuss and to write without the pressure of assignments for which they receive specific compensation or grants.

The members of the faculty as individuals are the point of educational influence on the student in classrooms, in the laboratory, in study conference. They are the critical element in the educational program of the college, and except for compensation, they have been given the honor and facilities that are appropriate to their high and essential function.

The members of the faculty *as individuals* must be distinguished from the faculty *as a body*. In the faculty as a body, an institutional framework and power is brought into being that serves badly the chief purpose assigned to it, namely, the design and administration of a liberal curriculum.

III

Since the liberal college is an instrument of liberal education, its essential activity is the promotion of learning. This activity is carried on through many programs of teaching and research by selected and authorized individuals who collectively are the faculty of the college. The research activities which are fostered by the college are for the most part individual programs initiated and carried on by individual members of the faculty and for which, as individuals, they are directly responsible. Cooperative research programs are not uncommon, particularly where unusual expense for apparatus or for assistance is called for, or where special requirements of investigation indicate a desirable pooling of interest and effort.

The teaching program of a liberal college is not, and cannot be, a matter for determination by each individual member of a faculty. Consequently, the liberal college has a plan or program of instruction, containing requirements, options and elections, leading under specified conditions to one or more publicly awarded degrees, which the college has power under its charter to grant, and for which the Trustees are responsible. The program leading to the degree is the curriculum, and for this, too, the Trustees are responsible, since it is by the quality and test of the curriculum that the degree is awarded. In general practice, the design and the operation of the curriculum have been referred by the Trustees to the faculty and other academic officers, but although the activities relating to the curriculum pass for the time being into other hands, the responsibility remains with the Trustees, who have the degree-awarding power.

IV

The curriculum of a liberal college is intended to be its principal instrument for the advancement of liberal education. The choice by the Trustees of the *collective* faculty as the agency for the design and administration of the college's curriculum is a particularly unfortunate one.

The liberal college faculty *as a body* is not competent to make the judgments and evaluations required to design a curriculum in liberal education. The individual members of the faculty are for the most part chosen as specialists in departmental subjects, and as a result both of knowledge and personal interest each is a special advocate, necessarily and desirably so. A collection of special advocates cannot be expected to be a repository and a voice of judicial wisdom.

The curriculum of a liberal college must always be the result of affirmative selective choice, of emphasis and of elimination—not all that is good can remain. The part must be judged against the whole. And change from time to time is imperative. The Trustees of a college choose unwisely when they refer the problem of curriculum for decision to the corporate faculty. They choose unwisely, and yet the responsibility for the curriculum still remains of necessity with the Trustees.

The fact that immediate control over the design of the curriculum is in the hands of the faculty has consequences of the most far-reaching character for the quality of the liberal educational program of the college and for its efficiency. And in view of the present public tendency to turn to the liberal college as a source of wisdom on matters affecting liberal education, weakness at this point is a matter of national concern.

The character and quality of the curriculum is directly, but of course not exclusively, affected by the balance of power within the faculty's specialized departmental structure. The departmentalized structure gives a prevailing and powerful vocational bias. It stimulates recruiting and the offering of highly specialized content courses attractive to a highly specialized student constituency. As a consequence, there is a pervasive deterioration of instruction that should be of a general and liberal character. Too often the importance of a course to the curriculum is determined by departmental voting strength in faculty meetings. Decisions are necessarily arrived at by *Robert's Rules of Order*, not by the Rule of Reason. Too often the dominant motivation is to advance and protect the professional status of the department and its subject matter, not the liberal education of the student.

The result is that the curriculum is of low quality judged by any standard by which one would evaluate an authentic liberal educational program, wisely founded on today's past and projected as best can be into today's uncertain future. It is of low quality judged by the high individual teaching competence of most members of the faculty. They do not look to teaching performance for professional advancement, for they are rarely so judged.

The prevailing attitudes of faculties in these respects are dealt with in Part 4 of this Report. *Achievement of the Possible.*

Bad as the quality of the liberal college curriculum is, its efficiency is even worse. The damage done to the liberal college by its economic poverty is beyond all estimation. The average salaries of members of the faculty are half or less what they should be by past standards and by present competitive necessity. To try to meet the situations caused by financial inadequacies, administrative officers and glamour professors must be on call to impress officers of foundations, influential alumni, the rich potential donor, the corporate contributor with an eye on next year's recruiting program, and preparatory school sources for next year's tuition-paying students. And publicity, always publicity.

V

The most serious general problem facing the colleges is the prevailing low level of academic salaries. This is a matter to which Trustees must give their profound attention in meeting their charter responsibilities.

Not only is the particular liberal college involved, but the national welfare itself is dependent in no small measure on obtaining from each generation an adequate participation of its able people in scholarship and research in academic institutions, as well as in the specialized professions, in commerce and in industry. Boys and girls in their years of vocational decision must be able to choose and prepare for academic careers with the knowledge that talent and effort will bring a success as rewarding, when everything is taken into account, as law, engineering, medicine, government or business. Today, the many appealing features of academic life are submerged by the fact of insufficient financial compensation.

The public has accepted without protest policy statements calling for at least doubling present average academic salaries. Concretely, this means a wide distribution of competent academic personnel in the salary range of $20,000 to $30,000.

The present salary scale is not only unjust to present faculty members, particularly those of longest standing and highest rank, but it prevents them from restoring through travel and study the inner resources of wisdom and enthusiasm on which the best teaching depends. The character of the liberal college, now and for the future, is being weakened, and the influence for good of the liberal college on liberal education is thereby diminished.

The Trustees may respond that they would like to see a drastic increase in academic salaries. But they ask, "Where is the money coming from?" The plain fact is that new money is not needed in anything like the amounts presently estimated. Many of the necessary funds are already at the disposal of the college or can be made so; but they are being dissipated through wastes in the curriculum, wastes in methods of instruction, wastes in administration and in the use of property and plant. Obviously the recoveries possible in the changes that will reduce these wastes will take a considerable period of time, with much planning, much patience and prompt action when the occasion is favorable.

There are three rough indicators by which the Trustees, the administration, the faculty and friends of the college can get a working idea of its over-all efficiency. A higher level of efficiency means better faculty compensation and all that goes with it; it also gives the potential for a teaching program that will turn out better graduates, although this can never be measured and will depend on influences outside the curriculum that mere efficiency does not touch.

These indicators are:

1. The ratio of students to members of the faculty.

2. The average number of hours per week that members of the faculty are engaged in lecturing, classroom or laboratory instruction.

3. The relation of aggregate faculty compensation to tuition income.

1. The ratio of students to faculty can vary within a wide range and is a matter of curriculum planning and curriculum administration. The idea that the lower the over-all ratio of students to teachers, the better the quality of instruction is sheer fantasy, although widely believed. Even the assumption that the lower the ratio of student to teacher in particular subjects, the higher the quality of instruction has never been substantiated. The feasibility of an over-all ratio of 20 to 1 is explored in Part 3 of this Report, Models of the Possible. Here it is shown that by the moderate use of the lecture and lecture-discussion methods wide latitude is given for seminars and even for authentic tutorials. For a college of 800 or more

students, an over-all ratio of 20 to 1 appears reasonable as an educational standard, and of course it is much more efficient than the practice prevailing today.

2. The number of hours spent on the average by members of the faculty in direct teaching of students in formal groups is an essential figure in the calculation of a college teaching program. In Part 3 of this Report a figure of 9 hours a week is taken for three of the models and 9⅓ hours for the fourth. The basis for these figures is that they conform to prevailing ideas of good practice and seem to make sense in that they give some 27 hours out of a 36-hour working week for the member of the faculty to prepare for direct instruction, to read student tests and papers and to meet a fair burden of student appointments. It must be remembered that this schedule applies for about 33 weeks of a year, and that major commitments of time for research should be provided by a research budget, not squeezed out of the teaching budget. It must also be remembered that a 36-hour working week is not excessive, and that other hours are available for reading, writing and conversation with colleagues.

Almost as important as average hours is the distribution of hours among members of the faculty and of the different departments. There will be appropriate variations, relating to methods of instruction, subject matter and duplication of offerings. But if unwanted courses or unneeded sections are preserved, they will distort the averages and must be eliminated from time to time.

3. A third highly important indicator is the ratio of total faculty compensation to tuition receipts. Administrators generally object to "tied revenues," and there is much to be said against this restraint on freedom of budgeting and freedom of action. Generally the difficulty arises when the "tied revenue" is in excess of the requirements of the expense to which it is tied, resulting in extravagance and waste. This difficulty can hardly arise realistically in the ratio of faculty compensation to tuition receipts.

It is desirable that the Trustees, after examining the record for a period of years—the last 10 at least—should set a goal percentage which will be something to shoot at. Whether the figure be 70% or 80% or 90% of tuition income, as long as it is somewhat higher than recent experience, it will serve important purposes in the operation of the college.

In the first place it will encourage the administration to look for new and additional sources of funds outside of tuition income. Not many institutions have organized their alumni giving to the level of productivity that can be achieved. In the second place it will be a strong restraint on the creeping expansion of administrative expense of all kinds, and of expense not related directly to faculty salaries or to the production of additional income. Such restraint is needed because of the direct access of the administration to the budget and to the Trustees.

Finally, and most important, a policy and a goal in allocating tuition receipts to faculty compensation will be a pledge to the faculty that economies that can be made in the design and administration of the curriculum will be reflected in additional faculty compensation, and not be diverted to administrative conveniences, or to an expansion of costly student activities, or avoidable buildings and grounds expenditures, or even to a reduction in the efforts to obtain current income from alumni and friends.

The ratio of faculty compensation to tuition income is not a precise index of educational efficiency, since even a 100% ratio can be frittered away in low student-teacher ratios without building faculty quality. Similarly, it would be undesirable to achieve a 100% ratio by depriving the student of proper teaching aids and a wholesome setting for his student life. But broadly speaking, a ratio of 50% must be regarded as an indication of doubtful educational merit and 60% as only a little better.

If, as a practical matter, the Trustees can look to the

achievement of a 100% ratio in a reasonable period of time, it is a goal worth setting, and it will be a stimulus to effort and planning by all who are associated with the college: Trustees, administration, faculty, alumni and friends. With 100% of tuitions going to faculty compensation, it can be said that every dollar paid by a student for tuition goes into direct faculty instruction. It means that the nontuition income—from Trustees, the alumni and friends of the college, the endowment and extracurricular activities—is sufficient to pay for the costs of administration, library, building maintenance, student activities and other overhead charges. In other words, the college has provided the setting for the student's education; the student pays only for his instruction.

VI

The weakness of the liberal college today and the measures both internal and external that must be taken to give the college the strength it badly needs require a change in the traditional management of the over-all program of the liberal college.

The Board of Trustees has in fact final responsibility under its charter for the educational program as well as for the property of its institution. Having final authority and responsibility, it also has accountability for a performance it is willing to defend to the state, to the national and local community, to donors of property, to parents and students, to the individual members of the faculty who have committed themselves and their families to an educational and intellectual program as their way of life.

The Trustees, therefore, must take back from the faculty *as a body* its present authority over the design and administration of the curriculum. The Trustees must take back this authority, but not because the Trustees *as a Board* are able to exercise it better than can the faculty as a body. True, the Board of Trustees is a smaller group than the faculty, and it has not ordinarily formed rigid and explicit vested interests in specific subject matter or ideological and methodological opinions divisively held. But these advantages which the Board of Trustees presently may have over the faculty as an agent for curriculum policy are of secondary importance and indeed might prove to be temporary.

Since the Trustees, as a Board, offer little if any more promise than the faculty, as a body, as an agency for the design and administration of the curriculum, but since the Board of Trustees does have the final authority and accountability, it must find, adapt, invent or create a new and suitable instrument through which the curriculum and methods of instruction may better contribute to the cause of liberal education. As Part 4 of this Report suggests, this new instrument may be the office of the President itself, reoriented, supported and held responsible for adequate curriculum performance. Or the new mechanism may be a rededicated, revitalized and strengthened Committee of the Faculty on the Curriculum. Or perhaps a new Council for Educational Policy and Program, including members of the faculty, the administration and the Trustees should be created.

What is needed is a break with traditional institutional history, plus the assurance that every individual member of the new mechanism is, so far as possible, knowledgeable as to the means and ends of liberal education and dedicated personally to the objective of forming this particular institution so that it may make its appropriate contribution to that purpose.

In selecting an instrument for the purpose of reconstructing the curriculum of a liberal college, the Trustees must keep in mind that the process will take many years of devoted work and that flexibility and adaptability to experience, to circumstance and to the unpredictable are necessary to avoid rigidity and the inevitable hostility that responds to a stubborn and arrogant force. Suggestions will come from many quarters, both from within and without the college; the President, however identified with the effort, will be a principal source of suggestion and criticism. Serious and sincere friends of the college, faculty and alumni and others will have special insights and prejudices that must be taken into account. Just as the instrument itself must be alert and flexible, so also must be the attitude of the Trustees toward its operation and evolution.

In the successful discovery and support of the organizational mechanism for authority over the curriculum best adapted to the traditions, personnel and potential resources of their own institution, the Trustees will safeguard and magnify the contribution of all liberal colleges to the public purpose of promoting the cause of liberal education.

PART 2

Curriculum and Methods
of Instruction

General

The liberal college makes its contribution to liberal education primarily by means of its curriculum.

Although the curriculum is the primary means whereby the liberal college expresses its liberal purpose, it is not the only means, and the other instruments available to the college need be noted, if only to avoid excessive emphasis on the curriculum as such. There are, of course, the extracurricular activities, organized and unorganized, traditional and spontaneous. The college can give direction to the trend of such activities and, to a significant degree, form them to strengthen its program of liberal education. The conditions of student living are matters of large concern for the residential college and are accepted as a residual responsibility by many colleges that do not offer board and room to all of their own. The uses of discipline and of freedom for students, and for faculty too, are matters of educational policy as well as of convenience.

Nor should we omit reference to the admission policies and all that goes with them, decisive in providing the individual cells from which the living body of the college is formed. Who should be admitted? Who should be permitted to remain? How should recruitment be handled? And then there are the alumni, their organization, their impact on the college and on public opinion. They are still a part of the college, and they affect the success of the college in its educational purpose.

The role of the President is most important in providing articulate leadership, initiative in the transforming of accepted tradition, protection against the conscious and unconscious dangers that bear in from friend and enemy alike, and, with all these overtones, in seeing to it that the ordinary day's business gets efficiently done, that the bills are paid, that the grass is cut and that the gates are locked at the proper time.

Curriculum

The number of courses, sections and units of instruction offered by the liberal college in its curriculum has increased greatly over the years. For a long time, this tendency to increase the number of courses was called "enrichment" and was considered a good idea. More recently such increase has been called "proliferation" and is no longer believed to be as good an idea as it once was.

Many reasons, rationalizations and excuses are given for the increase in the variety of courses offered. If the curriculum of 50 years ago had been perfect for then and for now, presumably mere increase in the size of the student body would not have required an increase in course offerings. To be sure, it was not perfect, and time has forced changes to take account of "now" as compared with "then."

One important explanation for the increase in course offerings has been the expansion of knowledge in the last half century. This is certainly valid for some part of the change, but it is not convincing as an over-all explanation.

Another factor has been the development of interdepartmental areas of interest, broadening what was narrow, relating what was isolated. This certainly has happened, particularly in the physical and social sciences.

Pressures from organized representatives of special professional and accrediting interests, local-community and regional groups have played their part. The demands of students and

parents are responsible for the addition of courses with vocational orientation and for novelty courses. Colleges have
also often added courses that only a few students asked for
and then have continued them after the demand was gone.

Each of these influences explains in part why the increase
in the number of course offerings took the particular form it
did, but all taken together they do not explain the size and
extent of the increase. As a matter of fact, the basis for the
growth was the doubling of the students coming to the liberal arts colleges, and the pressures from departments of the
faculties to increase even more the number on the teaching
staffs to serve them. This resulted in a drop in the student-
teacher ratio at the same time that the student body itself was
increasing. The college teacher naturally prefers to give his
own course under its own title just as soon as he can manage
to do so. The decisive pressure for increase in the number of
courses offered came from within the faculty itself and was a
response to inter- and intradepartmental competitive forces
that are understandable and real.

In addition to the increase in the variety and number of
courses offered, there has been an increase in the number of
"sections" into which students are divided for purposes of instruction. Sometimes the sections are simply divisions of one
course; sometimes the sections are associated with large lecture courses. No positive assertion can be made that the sectioning of instruction is in every case wasteful and unneces-
sary. No statistical evidence can be provided by studying
college catalogs, for although course offerings are listed, the
sections into which the students are divided often are not.
However, it is known from direct experience that a certain
amount of sectioning is deliberately organized as a make-work
device, and that the resulting instruction is on a recitation
basis unsuited to a college level of teaching. We also know
that the sections provided in connection with lecture courses
are frequently designed to reduce the number of lectures that

must be prepared and given and, at the same time, to evade the organized discussion that the skillful lecturer finds it possible to provide in every lecture—when the group is not too large and when the physical facilities permit.

A further cause of low student-teacher ratios is the large number of courses offered in which the registration is less than 5, or between 5 and 10. The course with small enrollment, properly used, has its valid place in a liberal-college curriculum. But such courses should be either of the seminar or the tutorial type, organized with teaching objectives in mind. The students, the instructor and the subject matter should in every case be capable of responding to this advanced and expensive form of instruction. When this is the case, it is not only proper for the college to offer this teaching method, it is its duty to do so. Unfortunately, too often the small course is an unplanned lecture or recitation experience, a residual offering from a previous departmental plan, a hope unrealized on the part of a faculty member not otherwise engaged. The small course must be carefully administered, and should be obliged to justify its place annually, to be sure that it makes its unique contribution to the liberal curriculum.

Methods of Instruction

The selection of the most effective and efficient methods of instruction is a matter of overwhelming importance to the liberal college since, at any level of tuition income, faculty salaries are sharply affected by how the curriculum is administered.

There are four main considerations bearing on methods of instruction: first, the academic calendar; second, the selection of ways of presenting the materials of instruction; third, the physical facilities available for instruction; and fourth, the experience, attitudes and talents of members of the faculty.

The Calendar

The academic calendar has two phases: (1) the organization of the academic week and (2) the organization of the academic year.

The academic week. The prevailing practice in organizing the academic week is to provide for 5 courses of 3 hours a week each, or 15 hours a week in the classroom for each student. Modifications are made for laboratory and field work, and special arrangements are sometimes made for very small classes and for independent study. If it is presumed that a student spends 2 hours out of class in preparation for each hour in class, the 15-hour week in class becomes a 45-hour student workweek applied directly to the subject matter of the curriculum.

It is a matter of common observation that only the rare adolescent undergraduate can so organize his week as to find 45 hours for attention to curriculum subject matter without severe and undesirable pressures on his health, his social life, his normal amusements, voluntary reading and relaxations. Consequently, the 45-hour workweek is not realistic and is compromised either by less outside study all along the line, or by the inclusion of at least one well-reputed "snap" course that can be passed either without much outside work or with a short period of final intensive cramming or tutoring.

Recognition of this situation has caused a number of colleges to limit the number of courses to 4 or even 3 instead of 5, with a resulting 12-hour class-week schedule instead of 15. It was also thought that simultaneous attention to 3 or 4 courses rather than 5 would be desirable. This change is made to bring about less scattering of the student's attention. Moreover, in the transition to fewer courses, it has been found that some courses formerly spread over 2 semesters could be consolidated in 1, with good educational advantage.

These changes in the academic class week, adopted on educational grounds, also have important economic and financial consequences. The student is now in class only twelve-fifteenths of the time spent formerly and, with proper organization and administration, the ratio of student to instructor can go up without any more time spent by the instructor in class. Reduction in the class week is probably the most immediate way of achieving a noncontroversial and important increase in the student-teacher ratio. Plans should be made to capture the benefits, lest they be dissipated in course proliferation, needless reduction in applied faculty hours or other wasteful practices in curriculum and methods of instruction.

The academic year. The present academic year for most liberal colleges is 33 weeks, consisting of 2 semesters of 16½ weeks of applied time plus two rather longish vacations of 10 days to 2 weeks each. A change might well take place following substantially the pattern set years ago by the University of Chicago, Stanford University, the University of Minnesota and a few others, where the 33-week year of 2 semesters was turned into three 11-week terms. The direct advantages are economy in the time allocated to examination periods and the fact that the Christmas holiday comes between two terms instead of in the midst of first semester as it does today under the 2-semester calendar.

A third important advantage is possible: a fourth 11-week equivalent term can be offered in the period which is now the summer vacation. This would make a working year of 44 weeks instead of 33. The faculty would still be on a 33-week year for full-time service, but the student could take 44-week years for a 4-year course. Or he could take 44 weeks one year and 22 weeks the year preceding or following if he wished to travel around the world or devote himself to some other experience.

This plan involves an initial burden on the faculty in that all courses must be reduced from about 15 teaching weeks (excluding examination periods) to 10. But once this task is completed, the new curriculum is in hand. And at one stroke the physical capacity of the plant is increased by one-third. The student body can also be increased by one-third without any increase whatever in the number of students on the campus at any one time. Finally, the individual professor has a choice, subject to the accommodation of other individual professors, of taking his annual leave in either summer, fall, winter or spring. This gives him four possible choices instead of one, makes possible the combined vacations of 2 years into 1, and provides flexibility not now practical in the academic schedule.

This 4-term calendar has economic advantages of great importance. First of all, gross dormitory rentals could be increased by one-third per annum. Second, with faculty cooperation on the scheduling of vacations and with success in maintaining a fairly even student load in each of the four terms, a one-third increase in tuition income is arithmetically possible. This could be done without increasing either the size of the faculty or the number of hours of teaching per week or year, provided the scheduling of courses results in an increase of one-third in the student-faculty ratio. Nor, as has been stated, would there be any increase in the number of students on the campus at any one time.

The economies available to a liberal college now on a 15-hour teaching week and on a 2-semester 33-week year, through changes in the weekly and annual calendar, and increases in the student-faculty ratio, provide the financial means for substantial salary increases. This does not count the additional new money from dormitory rentals.

The Organization of Instruction

From the economic point of view, the organization of instruction is essentially a matter of class size, that is, how many students a teacher can manage effectively for teaching purposes at one time. Given a certain number of hours that an instructor teaches, the higher the average number of students in a class, the lower the direct cost of instruction. The savings can be put into teaching salaries.

Instruction can be organized in several different ways, and the terms are rather loosely used. For the purpose of analysis, we may classify teaching groups as: (1) lectures, (2) lecture-discussions or small lectures, (3) seminars and (4) tutorials. The "section" is usually a section of something else and the teaching load involved must be charged against the teaching group of which it is a part. The big omission from the above list is the recitation, in which the instructor merely determines how well the student has memorized his assignment. From a pedagogical point of view it is out of place at the college, and, accordingly, it should be eliminated as an element in curriculum planning.

From the standpoint of size, these several methods of instruction may be classified as follows:

Lecture	80 to 400 or more, average 250
Lecture-discussion	25 to 150, average 75
Seminar	8 to 20, average 12
Tutorial	1 to 6, average 3

Other observers will place these figures differently, particularly the averages, which of course are subject to important variation both in reality and as ideals to aim at.

The lecture method of instruction should be used only when it is clearly a *good* method, considering subject matter, skill of the lecturer, objective of this particular course, maturity of the student body and the physical facilities that are available. It is commonly felt that the lecture is a poor substitute for a seminar or a discussion group. However, the lecture is a method of teaching that has its own place and, well done, has its own validity. It is resisted by many faculty members because they have had no training or experience in lecturing, and because lecturing is much more exacting than "handling" a class of 40 or less.

The great value of the lecture is that it creates a situation in which simultaneous mass communication may occur, in which the emotional component, if not too strong, will transform in meaningful ways the relations of partially related subject matter and will assimilate the transformation as mental stuff for new understanding and exploration.

The lecture-discussion or small lecture provides for a certain amount of student participation, under the affirmative leadership of the lecturer. Such groups may be effective with as few as 25, if the lecturer does not permit too much informality. They may be as large as 150 or even larger, given a lecture hall designed for the purpose and a lecturer who is technically a master of the method. A good average for the lecture-discussion is 70 to 80. Unfortunately, classrooms in academic buildings, having been constructed to handle the recitation method, are ordinarily too small and are badly arranged for the lecture-discussion teaching method.

The term "seminar" is used to cover a variety of methods of instruction for groups of between 8 to 20, with an average of 12. The essential element of the seminar, as we use the term here, is open discussion under relatively loose instructional leadership. It is not economical for groups of under 8 and is likely to get out of hand for groups larger than 20.

The tutorial method is used for groups of from 1 to 6, with an average of 3. It is a good method, it is an expensive method, and, well done, it is a fatiguing method. On the other hand, it is flexible, it requires fewer set meetings per week, and more independent reading. The instructor can use the tutorial class to help him with his own research. Because of its expense, the tutorial method should be used only when its justification is abundantly clear. It is economically practical when associated with a member of the faculty carrying a lecture, or a lecture-discussion group of average or greater-than-average size.

It is never a cheap method, no matter how immature and badly paid the tutors may be.

Much consideration has been given in recent years to "individual-study" plans, although, of course, this method of learning is older than the colleges and universities, and will be an important way of education for all strongly motivated students at all levels of natural ability. The "individual-study" plans become important for financial planning when they are substituted for regular units of the curriculum, and when the teaching staff is assigned to supervise these plans as part of, or in addition to, their regular teaching responsibilities. It is possible to associate these plans with the seminar or tutorial methods of instruction, but they are subject to extravagance and abuse—extravagance in making too much of the faculty's time available without standards of control, and abuse in giving the student academic credit for individual study without proper supervision and therefore with an inadequate service for his tuition payment.

Building Facilities

It goes without saying that the present classroom buildings of liberal colleges, not having been designed with the economic considerations of the college's educational program in mind, are rarely well suited for the purposes of an efficiently managed liberal education. Although for the most part they must be made to do, there are certain situations which justify corrective action.

If a college decides that it should and can increase its size (let us say from 800 to 1,200 students), and if it is in control of its curriculum, it would be prudent financially to borrow the money necessary for dormitories and to build efficient lecture facilities or remodel existing facilities. Science laboratories should be built only after the money is in hand, through gifts or earnings, not on speculation, since it is extremely difficult to estimate net cash return. Careful accounting should accompany all use of borrowed funds, particularly if the funds are borrowed from endowments. But the pitfalls of using borrowed funds should not be an excuse for holding back on a sound educational expansion that justifies itself financially as well as educationally.

Outlook

Each method of instruction based on class size has its pedagogical advantages, and in every case the larger the size, the more economical the program. The process of joining curriculum and methods of instruction must take place in the framework of a deep understanding of the college's own commitment to liberal education and a patient realization of how many years it will take to develop the program. There will be many compromises, and they should be accepted and turned to as good advantage as possible.

Basic trends are favorable to the liberal college that has achieved a minimum size of about 800 and that is prepared to grow. The population trend favors it; so does the trend of national income. Large resources will be available within the college's economic structure, and its competitive position, as compared to the university, will be advantageous in many ways. Finally, given proper compensation and a fair program for teaching, research and writing, the appeal of the liberal college to a distinguished faculty is very great. The outlook is for 20 or more liberal colleges of the highest quality within a period of 20 years or less.

However, if we take the college of below-average size—below the simple statistical average—the outlook is not good. Major and heroic labors will be required in reorganizing, refinancing and consolidation to preserve these many colleges, their services and their traditions.

PART 3
Models of the Possible

The potential financial strength of the liberal college enrolling 800 or more students is very great. This can be seen clearly if we study models of differing combinations of faculty, courses and students and observe the consequence on class sizes and possible faculty compensation.

Presented in this section are model structures for liberal colleges of four different sizes: 1,800, 1,200 and 800 students (each assumed to have a more or less conventional calendar), and a fourth college of 3,000 with a 3-term calendar. For each model there are two tables showing possibilities in the organization of class size and a third table showing the faculty salaries that could be attained with the curriculum so organized. Each model is subject to a wealth of variation, as the tables illustrate. In practice, many adjustments can and should be made to conform to traditions, objectives, availability of unusual talent or of special facilities and resources of every kind.

As is true of all model building, a few standard assumptions have to be made to give comparability and a frame of reference within which various combinations can be tried out.

The models are presented without discussion of subject matter or content of the courses that will be offered. There are innumerable possibilities, depending on the resources of the college—in faculty, library, laboratories, quantity and quality of student body—so that a choice of any one or several patterns would divert attention from the main point to be demonstrated, the actual variety of possible patterns soundly designed to serve the economic requirements of an adequate scale of faculty compensation.

The standard assumptions that are made for each of the four colleges are:

1. The colleges are 4-year liberal arts colleges.

2. Payments made by the students for room and board are sufficient to pay all costs allocated to dining halls and dormitories.

3. Scholarships are given out of funds specifically designated for this purpose by the source from which the funds came, and tuition income is credited with a full tuition payment from every scholarship student. This condition will be difficult for many liberal colleges to meet, but it will become easier in the near future as demand for admission increases. In the past, many colleges have used selective scholarships as a form of price cutting, since it is better financially for the college to have a student paying half or even no tuition at all than it is to have a vacant dormitory room.

4. For each of the four colleges for which models are shown, it is assumed that $800 per year per student is available from tuition or otherwise for the compensation of the faculty. From this is deducted an aggregate of 25%, to cover retirement and insurance provisions at about 15% plus an additional 10% for sabbatical-leave reserves, for reasons explained later in this section. These models are designed in every case so that of the tuition paid by the student, $800 goes directly to faculty compensation.

For the use of these models, to the extent that more or less than $800 per student goes to faculty compensation, the tables showing the distribution of faculty salaries can be adjusted accordingly. If the amount is $700, then a salary of $20,000 becomes $17,500; if the amount is $900, $20,000 becomes $22,500.

5. As has been stated, faculty salaries as shown in the tables are stated *after* deducting estimated costs to the college

of insurance and retirement annuity provisions and reserves set up for sabbatical leaves of absence. These costs will vary according to the policy of the institution, but they make a substantial difference between the cost of a faculty member to his institution and the amount of money he receives that is available for his own expenditure in any particular year. Although the retirement and insurance provision and the sabbatical reserve are highly advantageous to the individual and to the college, the difference between cost to the college and current salary paid to the individual is so large that the difference should be clearly understood. Furthermore, full participation in the sabbatical reserve may never come to any given individual faculty member, since it constitutes a leave of absence under varying conditions and is given primarily for the benefit of the college. The sabbatical leave would ordinarily not start to accrue until an individual is on permanent tenure. This fact is recognized in the tables by making deduction for sabbatical reserves in the gross amount of only 10% from tuition income presumably available for current faculty salaries.

6. A ratio of 20 students to the equivalent of each full-time member of the teaching staff in residence is assumed. Models using this ratio are consistent with good educational practice.

7. Full-time faculty teaching is taken as 9 hours a week in the classroom on the average for the first three models and $9\frac{1}{3}$ for the fourth. This teaching load has been selected as a desirable objective, and a higher load, while possible, would give very different models. For example, an average load of 10 hours a week would require about 10% less faculty than the numbers shown in the models.

8. The student's classroom load is taken to be 12 hours in the classroom per week for a period of about 33 weeks per year. This calendar for student load is selected on the educational grounds discussed in Part 2 of this Report.

9. Attention should be called to the fact that the models

do not include any financial provision for various facilities generally associated with the large lecture. In so far as there are expenses for mimeographing, audio-visual aids, assistance in the reading of term papers, etc., they are excluded on grounds later discussed in this section, namely, that for purposes of clear definition, the models deal only with faculty compensation. To the extent that some institutions or some lecturers feel the need for breaking the lecture group into smaller discussion sections, there must be a proration of the model, reducing the allocation provided for large lectures and assigning the proper charge against the available number of small-group seminars and tutorials.

Aside from these technicalities, the basic fact is that the number of large lecture groups in any of the models is so small (only 8 in the college of 800 and only 50 in the college of 3,000 students), and the gross tuition revenue produced by them is so large that any efficient aids that need to be provided can be financed without much difficulty either inside the model or outside of it.

Also to be remembered is the fact that the models provide adequate teaching salaries for a year's work that actually consists of only about 33 weeks of time in residence for teaching, and only 9 hours of teaching a week in the classroom. Accordingly, the servicing of the lecture-discussion, of which no faculty member need have more than one, should be organized in the teacher's time available for instruction. Looking at the week and at the year as a whole, this expectation does not unduly limit his time for research and writing. In a particular case, if a member of the faculty has exceedingly high research talents, he should be specifically relieved of part of his ordinary teaching load, and the expense should be borne by a research allotment outside the financial structure of the model.

10. No special recognition or allowance is made for recitation sections or discussion sections for courses with three large lectures each week. As indicated in Part 2, recitation

sections are inappropriate in a course of study at college level. Discussion sections often have merit, but they can be variously organized.

General Observations on the Models

1. With a student-teacher ratio of 20 to 1, it is possible to design a curriculum with a considerable variety of seminar and tutorial courses, a moderate use of the lecture, and considerable use of the lecture-discussion method—and to eliminate the conventional recitation.

Colleges illustrated by the models for 800 and 1,200 students indicate that a lecture course designed for each of the four classes (freshman, sophomore, junior and senior) as a whole is necessary to get reasonable variety in seminars and tutorials. Such lecture courses cannot be elementary departmental courses, nor vocational courses, nor loose orientation courses, since they must be required of every student. Properly designed and properly taught, these 4 courses will become the heart of the liberal education program of the college. The gross tuition from these courses will be very high, and the college can afford to assign its best talent and provide all necessary equipment to make them a success. In the design of these 4 courses, inter-institutional cooperation would be beneficial.

2. *The Salary Tables.* We have been puzzled in deciding how best to make allowances for retirement and insurance benefits and reserves for sabbatical years. These benefits are given in some measure by all colleges, but not uniformly. They are clearly a cost of the instructional staff and are directly related to total faculty compensation. What we have done, as we have said, is to set aside 25% of the $800 assumed to be paid by the students in tuition for retirement and sabbaticals. This percentage is large enough in most cases to cover also the cost of other fringe benefits provided faculty members (such as

faculty children's scholarships, subsidized housing, group insurance, etc.). The balance after this 25% deduction is distributed as a Table of Compensation. Although this deduction understates the possible salary scale for some colleges, it may overstate the scale in a few cases. This was thought preferable to overstating the scale generally, causing subsequent disappointments and misunderstandings. Even with this large deduction the possible scale looks satisfactory, with adequate minimums and possible maximums that should bring high talent into college faculties. The scale available to the college of 800 students is surprisingly good.

3. The models for all colleges of varying size show a large number of possible small courses, seminars and tutorials. This indicates that a variety and richness in course offerings can be preserved with a student ratio of 20 to 1. However, it must be realized that the availability of these many courses to any given individual is much more limited. On the average, a student can have only slightly more than one small course in each semester or term of his four years of study. This limitation need not be a hardship if the small course is of bona-fide seminar or tutorial type and places heavy emphasis on out-of-class reading and writing. The assumption is of course made that the lecture and lecture-discussion courses which constitute the balance of the student's curriculum will improve markedly in quality with better teaching, better facilities, and stronger emphasis on these methods of instruction.

The curricular offerings under any of the models will be somewhat smaller than they are today, but perhaps not dramatically so. On the other hand, the program of the student will be drastically changed; with talented instruction and reasonable motivation, it will be changed distinctly for the better. Let the richness of the educational experience be within the individual course, not within the range of departmental offerings. The student has just so much time anyway.

The Four Models

Of the four models—for 800, 1,200, 1,800, and 3,000 students—the one developed for the college of 1,800 students is taken up first. As might be expected, the college of 1,800 students gives greater flexibility in curriculum choices and a somewhat wider range of faculty compensation than do colleges of smaller size. By the same token, the college of 3,000 students gives alternatives not found in a college of 1,800 students. Our model of a college of 3,000 students departs from the other three models in that it takes a different calendar, namely, 3 terms of 11 weeks instead of 2 semesters of 16½ weeks. It also assumes a student week to consist of 3 courses meeting 4 times a week rather than 4 courses meeting 3 times a week. This difference in weekly schedule requires a slight difference in faculty teaching load; an average of 9⅓ hours a week in the classroom for the college of 3,000 students instead of 9 hours a week in the models for smaller colleges of 1,800 students, 1,200 students and 800 students.

MODEL 1 (1,800 STUDENTS)

Model 1 is designed for a college of 1,800 students. An income rate of $800 per student provides a total income of $1,440,000 available for faculty compensation with salary payments of $1,080,000, after allowing 25% for retirement annuities, insurance and sabbaticals.

The ratio of students to full-time faculty in residence is taken at 20 to 1, and, therefore, for 1,800 students, the number of faculty in residence would be 90.

The faculty load would be 3 courses or sections meeting for 3 hours each a week, a teaching schedule of 9 hours a week. Thus in *each* of 2 semesters, the 90 members of the faculty would offer a total of 270 courses or sections, or a grand total of 540 courses or sections for the year.

With 1,800 students each taking 4 courses, there would be 7,200 registrations of students in individual courses or sections per semester, or a total of 14,400 course registrations in a 2-semester year.

We now have the basic figures for the model for class size: 14,400 course registrations must be fitted into 540 courses and sections, taught by a faculty of 90. A possible combination of courses and students is shown in Table A.

Table A POSSIBLE COMBINATION OF COURSES FOR A COLLEGE WITH 1,800 STUDENTS (MODEL 1)

A courses: 20,	Large lectures averaging 200 students, with a range of between 150 and 300 students,	
	20 × 200 =	4,000 course registrations
B courses: 80,	Lecture-discussion averaging 75 students with a range of between 50 and 125 students	
	80 × 75 =	6,000 course registrations
C courses: 440,	Seminar-tutorial averaging 10 students, with a range from 3 to 24,	
	440 × 10 =	4,400 course registrations
Total: 540	Courses or sections	= 14,400 course registrations

Table B on page 35 shows a second possible combination of courses and students.

The Class-C courses are of particular interest, since it is widely believed that a student-teacher ratio of 20 to 1 means the elimination of the seminar-tutorial and the disappearance of personal contact between teacher and student. This apprehension, although justly present, is not supportable, as the following analysis shows:

From Table A, out of a total of 540 courses or sections offered in any one year, 440 can average 10 students, with sizes varying from 5 to 15 students. Here is a possible pattern:

160 courses or sections averaging 15 students,	= 2,400 course registrations
200 courses or sections averaging 8 students,	= 1,600 course registrations
80 courses or sections averaging 5 students,	= 400 course registrations

Total: 440 courses or sections   = 4,400 course registrations

This shows that 280 out of a total of 540 courses can be very small indeed. More than three-quarters of the courses offered in any year can average only about 10 students per course, and one-third of the students' classroom time can be spent in such courses. If desirable, additional student time can be allocated to small student-led discussion groups associated directly with large lecture courses.

Table B offers relatively more seminar-tutorial courses, but the average size is somewhat larger.

Table B ALTERNATIVE COMBINATION OF COURSES FOR A COLLEGE WITH 1,800 STUDENTS (MODEL 1)

A courses: 20,	Large lectures averaging 240 students, with a range of between 150 and 300 students,	
	20 × 240 =	4,800 course registrations
B courses: 40,	Lecture-discussion averaging 60 students, with a range of between 50 and 125 students,	
	40 × 60 =	2,400 course registrations
C courses: 480,	Seminar-tutorial averaging 15 students, with a range of from 3 to 24,	
	480 × 15 =	7,200 course registrations
Total: 540	Courses or sections	= 14,400 course registrations

Table C (page 36) shows a possible distribution of faculty compensation. Bear in mind that each category is an average and that allowance has been made already for retirement and insurance deductions and sabbatical reserves.

Salaries in the highest category could be increased further by expanding the number of faculty in the lower brackets of the scale, if institutional policy makes this desirable. The pur-

Table C   POSSIBLE SALARY DISTRIBUTION FOR A COLLEGE WITH 1,800 STUDENTS AND 90 FACULTY MEMBERS (MODEL 1)

Total faculty compensation:	$1,440,000
Less 15% for retirement and insurance benefits and 10% for sabbatical-leave reserve	360,000
Balance available for salary payments	$1,080,000
Distribution of faculty salaries	
20 averaging $ 7,500	$ 150,000
30 10,000	300,000
20 12,000	240,000
10 16,000	160,000
10 23,000	230,000
90 12,000	$1,080,000

pose here is to show that a college of 1,800 students can afford top talent without hardship at any level.

Table C provides a good academic salary scale, especially when it is realized that the allowances for retirement, insurance and sabbaticals have been deducted.

MODEL 2 (1,200 STUDENTS)

Model 2, the college of 1,200 students, has a limitation on its program not shared by the Model 1 college just discussed. In order to obtain latitude for its seminar and tutorial courses, the Model 2 college must confine its large lecture courses to subject matter of interest to all members of the student body of the same class. These lecture courses should not be of the elementary, vocational or loose orientation type. They must stand up qualitatively as the core of the college curriculum. For a liberal college, this may not be a bad requirement.

The college with 1,200 students would have 60 faculty members, on the basis of a 20-to-1 ratio. Tuition income at $800 per student would total $960,000 of which $720,000 would be available for salary payments. The number of courses or sections offered, figured at 3 per faculty member, would be 180 per semester or a total of 360 for the year. Course registrations, assuming 4 per week for 1,200 students, would be 4,800 each semester or a total of 9,600 for the year. A possible combination of courses and students is indicated in Table D.

Table D   POSSIBLE COMBINATION OF COURSES FOR A COLLEGE WITH 1,200 STUDENTS (MODEL 2)

A courses: 8,	Large lectures averaging 300 students	= 2,400 course registrations
B courses: 52,	Lecture-discussion averaging 75 students	= 3,900 course registrations
C courses: 300,	Seminar-tutorial averaging 11 students	= 3,300 course registrations
Total: 360	courses or sections	= 9,600 course registrations

Here again we find latitude for seminars and tutorials, but this is gained by restricting the number of large lectures to one each semester for the freshman, the sophomore, the junior and the senior classes. One-third of student time during the year is spent in Class C courses.

Another possible combination is in Table E.

Table E   ALTERNATIVE COMBINATION OF COURSES FOR A COLLEGE WITH 1,200 STUDENTS (MODEL 2)

A courses: 20,	Large lectures averaging 120 students	= 2,400 course registrations
B courses: 40,	Lecture-discussion averaging 60 students	= 2,400 course registrations
C courses: 300,	Seminar-tutorial averaging 16 students	= 4,800 course registrations
Total: 360	courses or sections	= 9,600 course registrations

This model shows that by increasing the size of the seminar-tutorial course, more flexibility can be gained in the large lecture offerings.

The possible salary schedule, shown in Table F, although the one shown here does not extend as high as the one given for a college of 1,800 students, is nevertheless a great improvement over present practice.

Table F   POSSIBLE SALARY DISTRIBUTION FOR A COLLEGE
WITH 1,200 STUDENTS AND 60 FACULTY MEMBERS
(MODEL 2)

Total faculty compensation		$960,000
Less 15% for retirement and insurance benefits and 10% for sabbatical-leave reserve		240,000
Balance available for salary payments		$720,000
Distribution of faculty salaries		
10 averaging	$ 7,500	$ 75,000
15	10,000	150,000
15	12,000	180,000
10	15,000	150,000
10	16,500	165,000
60	12,000	$720,000

This table provides for a somewhat lower concentration at the minimums and for more massing in the middle ranges. The policy expressed by this table may not be suitable for many institutions. A considerable turnover among the younger members of the faculty and a smaller proportion on permanent tenure is not without advantage.

MODEL 3 (800 STUDENTS)

The liberal college of 800 students can provide a curriculum and salary structure better than one might suppose. With a 20-to-1 ratio, this college would have 40 faculty members. With $800 tuition per student, there would be $640,000 available for faculty compensation, of which $480,000 would consist of salary payments. If the 800 students each took 4 courses per week, there would be 3,200 course registrations each semester or a total of 6,400 course registrations for the year. A possible combination of courses and students occurs in Table G.

Table G   POSSIBLE COMBINATION OF COURSES FOR
A COLLEGE WITH 800 STUDENTS (MODEL 3)

A courses: 8,	Large lectures averaging 200 students	= 1,600 course registrations
B courses: 32,	Lecture-discussion averaging 50 students	= 1,600 course registrations
C courses: 200,	Seminar-tutorial (range from an average of 10 to an average of 25) averaging 16 students	= 3,200 course registrations
Total: 240	courses or sections	= 6,400 course registrations

Note that in this model for the college of 800, large lectures must be taken by all students, one each semester. Also note that the provision for very small tutorials is somewhat less generous than in the college of 1,200. Nevertheless, this limitation is offset by the salary scale of the faculty, which compares favorably with the larger college.

Another distribution of courses would be as shown in Table H.

Table H   ALTERNATIVE COMBINATION OF COURSES FOR
A COLLEGE WITH 800 STUDENTS (MODEL 3)

A courses: 12,	Large lectures averaging 200 students	= 2,400 course registrations
B courses: 28,	Lecture-discussion averaging 50 students	= 1,400 course registrations
C courses: 200,	Seminar-tutorial averaging 13 students	= 2,600 course registrations
Total: 240	courses or sections	= 6,400 course registrations

Model 3 has a range of average salaries from $7,000 to $18,000, after allowing for retirement and insurance deductions and sabbatical-leave reserves. Before such deductions—assuming the benefits were distributed equally—the range of average salaries would be $9,333 to $24,000 with top compensation (including the value of such deductions) in excess of $25,000. And this in a college of 800 students with $800 tuition per student going to faculty compensation! The details are in Table I.

Table 1 POSSIBLE SALARY DISTRIBUTION FOR A COLLEGE WITH 800 STUDENTS AND 40 FACULTY MEMBERS (MODEL 3)

Total faculty compensation		$640,000
Less 15% for retirement and insurance benefits and 10% for sabbatical-leave reserve		160,000
Balance available for salary payments		$480,000
Distribution of faculty salaries		
5 averaging	$ 7,000	35,000
5	8,000	40,000
20	12,000	240,000
5	15,000	75,000
5	18,000	90,000
40	12,000	$480,000

MODEL 4 (3,000 STUDENTS)

Model 4 is a model for a college of 3,000 students.

A different calendar is assumed, namely a 3-term academic year of 11 weeks per term, a student load of 3 courses or sections per term, each meeting 4 times a week. Three thousand students taking 3 courses or sections each in each of 3 terms would involve 27,000 course registrations.

At a student-faculty ratio of 20 to 1, there would be 150 faculty in residence. The teaching load for the faculty is taken as 2 courses or sections for 2 terms and 3 courses or sections for 1 term, a total of 7 courses or sections per year. Since the courses meet 4 times a week, the average hours per week would be 9⅓ hours (7 × 4 ÷ 3 terms). The total offerings by the faculty would be 1,050 courses or sections, that is, 7 courses for each of 150 faculty members.

These 1,050 courses or sections offered must provide for the 27,000 course registrations. Table J shows the possibilities of offering courses of different types.

Table J POSSIBLE COMBINATION OF COURSES FOR A COLLEGE WITH 3,000 STUDENTS (MODEL 4)

A courses: 50,	Large lectures averaging 180 students =	9,000 course registrations
B courses: 100,	Lecture-discussion averaging 90 students =	9,000 course registrations
C courses: 900,	Seminar-tutorial averaging 10 students =	9,000 course registrations
Total: 1,050	courses or sections =	27,000 course registrations

Another possible combination is shown in Table K.

Table K ALTERNATIVE COMBINATION OF COURSES FOR A COLLEGE WITH 3,000 STUDENTS (MODEL 4)

A courses: 100,	Large lectures averaging 90 students =	9,000 course registrations
B courses: 200,	Lecture-discussion averaging 45 students =	9,000 course registrations
C courses: 750,	Seminar-tutorial averaging 12 students =	9,000 course registrations
Total: 1,050	courses or sections =	27,000 course registrations

These two tables suggest the variety of educational possibilities that can be expressed in the student course structure of a college of 3,000 students.

Table L   POSSIBLE SALARY DISTRIBUTION FOR A COLLEGE
WITH 3,000 STUDENTS AND 150 FACULTY MEMBERS
(MODEL 4)

		Range	
Total faculty compensation			$2,400,000
Less 15% for retirement and insurance benefits and 10% for sabbatical-leave reserve			600,000
Balance available for salary payments			$1,800,000
Distribution of faculty salaries			
60 averaging	$ 7,000	(6,000– 9,000)	$ 420,000
50	12,000	(10,000–14,000)	600,000
20	16,000	(15,000–18,000)	320,000
10	20,000	(18,000–24,000)	200,000
10	26,000	(24,000–30,000)	260,000
150	12,000		$1,800,000

Future Possibilities

The "models of the possible" for the four colleges presented show clearly that the potential financial strength of the
liberal college is very great. But this strength is not present in
the many institutions where the capacity to attract a student
body of at least 800 paying a charge that will yield about $800
per student per year for the costs of instruction either does not
exist or cannot be made to exist. On a numerical basis, this is
the great majority of American liberal colleges today. They
must grow in size and organize their curricula along the lines
outlined elsewhere in this report. But what if they choose to
remain small because of the values they see in a small, closely
knit body of students and faculty? Unless they have unusual
outside financial resources, in the long run they cannot have
a good faculty nor provide a liberal education of high quality
or offer a substantial variety of courses.

However, the demonstration of what is possible today

for many shows the direction that must be taken by all to capture in the future the new strength that will come from greatly increased demands for liberal-college education.

Other Costs and Revenues

The Trustees of the liberal college must not feel that all their financial problems will be solved with changes in the design and administration of the curriculum. The most that can be accomplished, and this is no small gain, is to correct in some important measure the deplorable level to which academic salaries have fallen. It is clear that this correction cannot take place merely by an attempt to raise new endowments, larger gifts or higher tuitions.

On the other hand, additional funds will be required, and estimates and programs should be the concern of every college President and every Trustee. In the first place, the percentage of tuition going into faculty salaries is too low for comfort in most colleges. New money or new administrative economies must be found to raise this percentage. In the second place, it may be necessary, or at least desirable, for many colleges to find scholarship or loan funds to replace general income now being used for student aid.

Each college must decide what portion of its expense it will charge to instruction. What about libraries, teaching aids, laboratory supplies? What about the gymnasium, the student union, the golf course? In this Report we have used the concept of "faculty compensation" as being the criterion to which tuition payments are related. Any other standard seems difficult to apply with the rigor that is necessary for the goal to be achieved. It is better to take a lower percentage than to have an ambiguous or shifting standard.

The principal regular source to which a college may look for nontuition revenue is alumni contributions. A number of colleges have been surprisingly successful in these efforts, and their methods are open for all to see. An annual alumni fund program requires leadership, organization and the spending of promotional money. Such promotional money may seem, and may be, quite large in the beginning; it should be charged directly against the alumni fund, and the final alumni contribution to the college should be a net figure. Only in this way are the campaign managers likely to have the resources necessary for wide coverage and permanent establishments.

Gifts from other individuals are to be expected and cultivated, but they are irregular and unpredictable. It is better that unplanned gifts not be used to meet the recurring expenses of the college. On the other hand, they need not be frozen as endowments, with only the income used.

The stronger liberal colleges, those which today are able to attract tuition-paying students and are also able and willing to use a large percentage of these tuitions for the costs of instruction, and who organize their curricular program so as to give compensation levels that are practical with a higher student-teacher ratio, can become educational institutions of absolutely first rank. They can be greater in power and service than any colleges we have yet seen. Their potential financial strength is sufficient to make them communities of the truly great minds of the generation. The liberal college may indeed provide the setting for a richer and more productive intellectual community than does many a great and largely professionally oriented university.

The competition between the colleges and universities for faculty will become acute, since the well-managed college will be at no financial disadvantage in its search for personnel. The college will want for its faculty the man who can teach and who can write. Even the very good research man, if unable to teach well, cannot earn in teaching the high salaries that will be common in the strong liberal college. And through faculties of this type in the liberal college we shall protect and advance liberal education at all levels.

PART 4

Achievement of the Possible

The models developed in Part 3 are intended to show that a combination of courses, students and teachers different from patterns prevailing today could have far-reaching consequences for the liberal college. The thesis is that faculty compensation could be dramatically improved if a college could approximate the model most appropriate for it; that college teaching could compete on reasonably equal terms with other professions if the models and their compensation patterns could be achieved in a considerable number of institutions; and that these things could be accomplished without impoverishing the curriculum and without introducing novel methods of instruction.

A model is an abstraction. It is useful in exciting the imagination and in helping us to see beyond present complexities and limitations to an ideal design for the future. Even with the most faithful attention to the model and with the most dedicated effort, the reality will necessarily fall short of the ideal. But without any model as an objective and without sustained and energetic effort to make it a reality, unplanned and undirected change is not likely to lead to acceptable solutions for the most perplexing problem facing the liberal colleges.

Achievement of the possible requires planned change at the very heart of the enterprise. In a college, as in any complex organization of human beings, the orderly transformation of activities according to plan is not easy. Not all can agree on the wisest course to pursue, and usually a minority will oppose any significant change. In this regard, a college faces distinctive problems. It is a self-governing institution in which the authority to legislate on matters of educational program is in practice usually delegated to the faculty. The processes by which educational policies are formulated, deliberated and decided are essentially legislative and therefore political. While the determination of these matters is the most basic activity of the faculty acting in its collective capacity, the generally prevailing philosophy and power structure obstructs and frustrates it in the discharge of this vital responsibility. Moreover, once decisions on major issues are made by a majority, any plan will remain simply a blueprint unless individual teachers and groups of teachers are personally committed to it and work conscientiously and energetically for its realization. Cherishing the principles of equality and freedom of dissent, the liberal college does not readily discipline those with contrary views. In the final analysis, therefore, the success of a plan depends upon informed, dedicated and persevering support. For all of these reasons, planned change in a college is more difficult to achieve than in many other stable organizations.

Ways and means of effecting change in the liberal college is the concern of this chapter. Satisfactory treatment of the subject is not easy. For one thing, thoughtful observers are only beginning to interest themselves in the general problem of controlling change in stable organizations. Lacking precise knowledge, analysis of the problem must be based on insights drawn from observation of colleges and universities as they have undertaken to define their purposes, plan improvement of their performance, and put these plans into effect. Still another problem is posed by the complexity of the American system of higher education. There are nearly a thousand liberal arts colleges, several hundred professional and technical schools, and more than a hundred universities with clusters of schools, colleges and institutes. Every one of these institutions has its own traditions and habits, arrangements and practices. Each has its particular problems and each is changing in its own way. In all this variety there are doubtless common elements. But who can say what they are?

These difficulties notwithstanding, it may be useful to venture some generalizations, helpful at least in focusing attention on the problem. The observations which follow are concerned first with the political and administrative structures and processes by means of which decisions about curricula and teaching are made; second, with attitudes toward change; and finally, with the problem of organizing for change.

The College as a Government

I

An analysis of the college as a government may begin with some observations about institutional leadership. Viewed in the perspective of the past hundred years, it is obvious that the demands on the leadership of the American college have become increasingly burdensome. In the early nineteenth century the college was a simple organism. For the student the curriculum was essentially prescribed and was largely designed to prepare him for the learned professions. Enrollments were low and the students, although quite ready to riot and to harass teachers and presidents, seem in retrospect to have expected relatively little of the institution except the privilege of learning. The day-to-day problems, for the times no doubt perplexing, were readily manageable. The faculty was small and bonded together by common interests. Its administrative duties were not onerous and generally were handled in meetings of the entire faculty. The President expected as a matter of course to continue his teaching and scholarly activities. Initially an "equal among equals," upon election to the presidency he was still regarded as a colleague, although now the "first among equals." His duties did not take him away from the

campus for extended periods, and he did not need a comple-
ment of aides to handle administrative affairs. Because "administration" had not yet become a highly specialized function,
there was a minimum of the "we" and "they" approach in the
faculty's thinking about the institution.

In short, the college was a unit. It was held together by a
clearly perceived and accepted purpose, by a coherent curriculum, and by professional and social relationships in which sim-
ilarity of training, interests and institutional roles served as a
cohesive force.

The unity of the early nineteenth-century liberal college
began to break down with the industrialization and urbaniza-
tion of American society. Of the many influences contributing
to this change, perhaps three were decisive: the specialization
of knowledge and of its pursuit, the introduction of the elec-
tive system, and changes in the motivation for "going to college." Larger enrollments required larger faculties, which
increasingly were being trained in American universities. As
graduate students, teachers were exposed to new, specialized
subjects which they asked to have incorporated in the departmental structure of the college. Thus, "natural history" was
divided and subdivided into departments of geology, biology,
botany, zoology. Physics and chemistry, economics and political science—these and other disciplines split off from parent
departments. Moreover, within each department specialties
and subspecialties eventually were represented by faculty appointments and course offerings. The enrichment of a curriculum that too long was limited to subjects considered appropriate to an eighteenth-century education was certainly desirable. But in the process an ordered hierarchy of subjects
was replaced by a wide variety of courses whose relative
value for the student was determined primarily by his own
choices. Moreover, student course elections were no longer
guided by the needs of a few learned professions. The liberal
college was drawing its students from an increasing variety of

cultural backgrounds, while at the same time a growing urban, industrial society offered new and varied career possibilities. Many students went to college more interested in a degree than in the education which the degree symbolized, and more interested in the vocational usefulness than in the liberal content of courses. The curriculum was fragmented by this combination of forces.

Traditional arrangements for the government of the colleges also were under stress. For one thing, the college faculty was becoming too large and diverse to conduct much of its business in general faculty meeting. Various representative devices, especially elaborate committee structures were incorporated into faculty government. More and more faculty affairs were initially considered, if not finally settled, by committees. From the viewpoint of faculty participation in the government of the college, these devices no doubt were preferable to the alternative of having the faculty become less and less influential in the affairs of the college. But the result was not all gain. Faculty time and energy otherwise available for teaching and scholarship were diverted to committee service, much of it routine in character. And the sense of the faculty as a unitary, corporate entity was weakened.

The college presidency was influenced by these developments. The weakening of the faculty's capacity for self-government placed a heavier burden upon the central academic leadership of the institution. But with the growth in size and complexity of the college, its administration became more difficult. The President turned over to colleagues the administration of the library, the admission and registration of students, and disciplinary and other student problems. The larger and more varied college required a different kind of plant. Specialization affected the library almost immediately, and the new emphasis on scientific training required expensive laboratories. Finances, always a problem, required increasing attention. The President took on new assistants to help with such matters as the institution's finances and management of the plant. Some of his new activities required him to be away from the campus for extended periods. Under the pressure of his heavy duties, it was difficult for him to continue teaching and scholarship. He relied increasingly upon administrative subordinates and in the process found that a considerable part of his working day was spent with them. As in any complex organization—and the college was becoming complex—the adjustment and accommodation of competing and conflicting interests became a major concern of the chief executive.

What was the effect of these developments on presidential leadership? In larger institutions, at least, the President became somewhat remote from the day-to-day interests of students and faculty. It was necessary for him to exercise his leadership indirectly, through other people. But none of his aides could speak with his authority and prestige. On many campuses the result was a diffusion and weakening of the impact of leadership.

In short, the two central developments seem to have compounded the difficulties. The faculty and curriculum were fragmented by specialization and departmentalization. Strong leadership was needed to direct and control the forces at work, to blend the elements of new and traditional strength without yielding essential character. A greatly strengthened presidency might have met this need, as indeed it was met by exceptional men at various times in various institutions. In retrospect, however, it appears that the President's responsibilities grew too rapidly to be manageable, concurrently with the disappearance of a coherent curriculum and a unified faculty.

II

Government in a college has special problems resulting from the nature of the community. The college community is characteristically democratic and individualistic. The individual teacher's role is central to the integrity of the enterprise. In an ultimate sense, achievement of the organization's objectives rests upon the talent, effort and contribution of the individual faculty member. The purpose of the liberal college cannot be accomplished without good teaching. Good teaching depends upon the freedom of the individual teacher to pursue in the treatment of his subject his own ideal relationship with his students; to seek the truth for himself and others as he sees it, without fear except of error. And it depends upon the teacher's being motivated by these ideals in his relationship with his students, the institution and society.

The teacher is deeply individualistic in his attitudes toward regulation of educational affairs. He seems instinctively to resist organized authority when it is concerned with curriculum and teaching. If there must be controls, let them be democratically imposed and administered. In this area, "that government is best which governs least" is a basic tenet.

The institution itself recognizes the fundamental necessity of freedom for the teacher. It professes its belief in the freedom to search for and teach the truth, and to protect this freedom it confers the high privilege of permanent tenure upon teachers who have demonstrated their worth. By conferring this status, it reinforces, in the psychological sense, the teacher's preference for individualistic behavior. Once permanent tenure is granted, the teacher's relationship to the college community ordinarily is severed only when he reaches the established age of retirement. His behavior may be irresponsible, offensive, or even wrong as measured by the standards of a community of scholars; but unless he grossly offends the larger community, he is not likely to be disciplined by his faculty peers or by the President and Trustees. In short, individualism is not only condoned by the college community; it is encouraged and protected, because without it the institutional purpose cannot be fully accomplished. Short of gross offense, the restraints upon the individual teacher are chiefly those imposed by his own judgment, self-discipline and integrity.

A college is a community as well as a collection of individuals. If one seeks to identify the center of political power in this community, it is apparent that today the locus is the departments of the faculty. The departmentalization of disciplines is characteristic of American colleges and universities and is present to a greater or lesser degree in all institutions. It may be found in its most extreme form in large universities. In small colleges this development may be much less marked. This discussion describes in general terms the structure and functioning of the departmental system without attempting to isolate characteristics common to all institutions irrespective of size. The departments represent the disciplines in which members of the faculty are trained and by the development of which they obtain their greatest recognition and personal fulfillment. It is normally with departmental colleagues that members of the faculty have most of their working relationships. The department is the mechanism through which professional needs are met and professional standards are enforced. Often it is also the most rewarding social group to which the faculty member belongs. These relationships are recognized and strengthened by the custom of having members of a department housed in adjacent offices in the same building.

Within the departmental structure individualism is dominant. This tendency can be moderated by a respected, wise and permanent departmental chairman. The faculty usually prefers to have the departmental chairmanships on a rotating rather than permanent basis. Whether rotating or permanent, the function of the chairman as viewed by other members of the department is essentially that of a presiding and executive officer. His responsibility is to carry out the decisions reached by majority vote and to negotiate as successfully as he can with others whose cooperation and acquiescence are necessary to accomplish the department's wishes. He usually accepts the position, not because of the power it confers, but out of a sense of duty or because it carries prestige in professional and social relationships. There is at least this compensation for doing the departmental chores. Customarily the chairman's term is limited. Within his term, however, he is expected by departmental colleagues to carry out their decisions faithfully and by his administrative superiors to persuade his colleagues to accept decisions which may be contrary to their view of the department's immediate interests. His position is therefore one of tension. He must satisfy his departmental colleagues and also the administrative officers, who necessarily represent broader institutional interests.

His role as a college administrative officer is made more difficult by the democratic basis on which most major departmental decisions are made. When deciding matters of educational policy, the votes of the youngest members generally count as much as those of the most senior members. It is generally considered proper, however, to limit participation in personnel decisions to those above the rank of the person whose appointment or promotion is being decided. Even a permanent chairman is expected to be guided by his colleagues, and no chairman can take lightly their recommendations. If the department is large, its affairs may be in the hands of departmental committees to whom the chairman is expected to look for decisions on crucial matters. In the allocation of departmental teaching resources the chairman's role is influential but not decisive. He negotiates class schedules and course assignments, giving due weight to the preferences of senior colleagues for particular courses and hours.

In scheduling departmental offerings, the desire of junior members to have their own courses is a matter of constant concern. The institution probably has the "teacher-scholar" as an ideal image, and a faculty member may be a more productive scholar if his teaching, writing and research are closely allied.

If he has been brought in to help with a sectioned course, he has a strong case for at least one course of his own simply to relieve monotony. He is likely to be more effective if some course which he teaches is of special interest to him. If he is not given such a course, he may leave. It would be at least a bother to find a replacement, and the President and dean may be reluctant to allow the department to fill the vacancy. A reduction in the size of the department might increase the load of the remaining members. Since the standing of the department on and off campus tends to be a reflection of its size, there is steady attention to the question of enrollment. The more varied, dramatic and apparently practical the course offerings, the greater the possibility of attracting students. The larger the enrollment, the stronger the case for additional faculty appointments.

These considerations—the department's interest in enrollments and expansion, the continuing fragmentation of disciplines by ever greater specialization and the usefulness of combining teaching and research—all contribute to the tendency to add courses to the departmental curriculum. Other factors are significant. For many students, a college education is preparation for graduate or professional school. These schools usually have definite ideas about the courses which best prepare students for subsequent study, and these ideas are influential in shaping the college curriculum. Professional and accrediting organizations seldom limit themselves to mere suggestions, and their interests extend to the adequacy of facilities, faculty salaries and teaching loads, and even to matters of internal organization. Also, it seems to be true that as a college grows in enrollment its offerings tend to become more specialized and numerous. Finally, all of these factors are compounded if an institution views itself as a place where almost any person may go to receive instruction in any subject.

The political situation in the department does not provide any serious impediment to these tendencies. The provision of satisfactory outlets for the interests of individual members of the department is both a matter of mutual adjustment of interests among colleagues and of persuading institutional elements outside the department to accept the department's wishes. In this context, the proposal to add a new course to the departmental offerings is likely to be considered chiefly in terms of the prospect of its being approved by faculty committees responsible for changes in course offerings. The demand which one new course makes upon the institution's resources ordinarily is not great, particularly if the teacher is already on the staff, the personal and professional interests of a colleague are compelling, and other departments are adding courses to their offerings for no better reasons. The usual, predictable result is departmental approval of a colleague's proposal of a new course. And so the curriculum grows.

III

When depicted on an organization chart, a college resembles any other institution following the hierarchical pattern. The Governing Board is shown at the top of the triangle, with the President reporting to the Board. Under the President are the various administrative officers who report to him. The administrative officer responsible for academic affairs has grouped under him the various departments of instruction. The chain of command runs from the Board to the President to the academic dean, thence to the chairmen of departments, and ultimately to the individual teacher. As in other bureaucracies, there is a division of labor based upon specialization. The members of the organization are chosen because of their professional competence. The faculty members, at least, are not subject to arbitrary dismissal, and they are careerists. If they do not have permanent tenure in the institution, they have at least committed themselves to the profession and aspire to permanency in some college or university. They are the permanent civil service without which the college cannot do its job. In all of these respects the college resembles the bureaucracy of government, military, religious and business organizations.

On close examination, however, the reality is found to be quite different. The "chain of command" in a college is at most a tenuous line of influence. The President and deans must rely primarily upon departmental chairmen to direct and influence the departments. But, as already noted, the chairman's ability to meet this expectation is based upon a delicate and unreliable relationship. He does not have the sanction of dismissing recalcitrant colleagues. In carrying out institutional policies, he requires strong backing from the President and dean, and he must depend largely upon his skill as a negotiator and upon his ability to persuade colleagues that the decision is at least pragmatically right and that acceptance is in the long-run interests of the department. When matters of staffing, of curriculum and of teaching methods are involved, a department's capabilities for resistance are almost unlimited. Its members are protected from summary dismissal, and often a majority are on permanent tenure. Academic freedom and the sanctity of the classroom give philosophical and practical support to a policy of resistance. Moreover, the spirit which the teacher brings to the classroom is uniquely important. What he does not do enthusiastically, he does not do well. To impose upon him a change in curriculum or teaching method which does not evoke his enthusiasm is self-defeating. His teaching is likely to be less effective than it was before the change.

IV

For this reason it is essential that significant change be supported by a substantial majority with informed understanding of weaknesses in the present situation and with considerable enthusiasm for the venture. In the usual college community, the committee system is widely used to obtain this support. Committees are constituted with due regard to the necessities of representing various points of view and interests. This feature is particularly notable in committees responsible for educational and personnel policies. A standing committee of the faculty charged with the responsibility for educational policy usually does not have authority to put its proposals into effect. It is expected to study, to report periodically, and to formulate proposals for consideration by the faculty. Under these circumstances it is not surprising that the committee has difficulty in separating its concern for what *should* be done from considerations of political feasibility.

Sitting as a legislative body in general faculty meeting, the faculty is a collection of specialists whose analytical and critical talents are highly developed by training and daily exercise. Discussion of a committee report on a complex problem provides an almost irresistible opportunity for critical minds. It is also an opportunity to demonstrate one's superior intelligence, wit and wisdom. Jousting with committee members enlivens a meeting which might otherwise be deadly. However hard it has tried to accommodate known viewpoints, on major issues a committee usually cannot count upon the help of a "pro-committee" party. There is no disciplined group that can be held together by the committee in support of its proposals. If, as is customary, the President or other administrative officers are members of the committee, the report may win some support from faculty members who are generally sympathetic with "the administration" and who believe that the President favors the proposal. But an equal number of negative votes may be cast because the proposal *is* identified with the administration. The tendency of members of American college and university communities to be classified as either "faculty" or "administration" is well known. This "faculty-administration" dichotomy makes it difficult to think of the college as an enterprise in which both groups have a common interest and to the advancement of which both are dedicated.

In the daily life of the institution, the "faculty-*vs.*-administration" attitude can be irritating to both groups without being serious for the institution. When it finds expression in legislative sessions of the faculty, however, the "anti-administration" viewpoint may be decisive in the outcome of a committee proposal affecting vital institutional interests. There is little that the President can do to meet this opposition. He has at best only limited patronage, and wisdom suggests that he refrain from using it. He cannot appeal over the heads of the faculty to a common constituency in the next election. He might withhold salary increases from "anti-administration" colleagues, but to do so for this reason would be wrong and possibly disastrous.

A proposal for a radical change in the curriculum faces an even greater difficulty. It has already been noted that the department is the nucleus of power in the college political community. When departmental interests come into play, the political behavior of the faculty may begin to resemble that of a confederation of independent sovereignties, each with national interests to protect. Questions of jurisdiction, procedure and protocol assume an importance that at times outweighs the substantive issues. The experience of many institutions indicates that this tendency can be overcome through leadership which by one means or other creates a sense of common cause and institutional interest transcending all else. The loyalty and dedication of the individual faculty member to education and to the institution is always on call. But experience also indicates that there are formidable obstacles to this result.

For one thing, there are no competing political parties to vitalize and guide the legislative function. The legislative body is composed of individuals who have professional and personal interests in many of the matters being decided. Moreover, these individuals are not personally answerable for decisions affecting the institution. Under these circumstances, the perception of a general, institutional interest, as distinct from special and

departmental interests, is extraordinarily difficult. So constituted, a faculty is not organized to exercise effectively and ob-
jectively its corporate responsibility to formulate and maintain an educational program based on general rather than
special interests. In short, the structure impedes rather than
aids the making of responsible institutional decisions.

Attitudes toward Change

In addition to the organizational and political factors de-
scribed in the foregoing section, faculty members as individuals are likely to be slow to accept change in the educational program. Some of these attitudes may be insignificant
in a given situation; others may be so basic that little can be
done to influence them. Those who hope to bring about radical
change in a college should have these attitudes in mind.

I

In spite of all that has been said and written about the
very serious plight of the liberal college, there is little real appreciation among individual members of the faculty of the
urgency of the problem. The deterioration of the economic
status of the teaching profession has been gradual and is not
perceptible to any one generation. Educational and public
leadership has not been able to convey in terms meaningful to
the college teacher a conviction that there is a deep national
interest in reversing the process of professional deterioration.
In a crisis men may accept willingly change which normally
they would oppose. But the present "crisis in American higher
education" is reassuring to the teaching profession. There is a
greater demand for education than ever before. The teacher
is a valuable commodity in short supply. Consequently, in a
highly competitive market he can expect to increase his compensation without any increase in productivity. In fact, a reduction in teaching load may be offered, as well as a salary in-

crease, to entice him to another institution. Moreover, throughout the nation it is recognized that teachers' salaries are disgracefully low. It is admitted that this country is not putting enough of its resources into its educational system. And it is argued that the cost of a college education is a capital investment which the student and his family should pay in full, over a period of years if not currently. These and related views help create the impression that the problem will be solved regardless of what the teacher does or does not do.

It might be noted, also, that the American Association of University Professors—the principal national association representing teachers and scholars rather than disciplines or institutions—has not assumed leadership in counteracting this view. It is working energetically to bring about improvement in faculty salaries and in other aspects of employment. But there is little indication that it believes that the profession is obligated to contribute to the solution of the salary problem by eliminating waste in present curriculums and teaching methods. Thus the individual's attitude toward change is reinforced by the national organization which seeks to represent and advance his interests.

II

The individual faculty member usually does not have basic information about the way the teaching resources of the institution are being used. If information about teaching loads, course offerings and enrollments is available to administrative officers, it is not likely to be distributed routinely to the faculty. Lacking this basic information, it is small wonder that the individual teacher does not see the possibilities of improving his economic status by means of an institutional program utilizing total faculty resources more efficiently. Moreover, significant progress depends upon collective rather than individual action. The individual who recognizes the problem may feel impotent to do anything himself to solve it, and from previous experience he may well be skeptical about the possibilities of cooperative action.

III

Then, too, the average faculty member is likely to be quite conservative about educational matters. The status system is a conservative influence. The younger members of the faculty might be expected to provide the impulse for change. But their retention and advancement in the institution rest largely on the favorable judgment of their departmental seniors. Until the young teacher has made a firm place for himself in the department, it is natural for him to be cautious about stirring things up. In any event, the "innovators" in life are relatively few. The status quo has at least the advantage of being known. Particularly with respect to specialization in the curriculum and departmentalization of the faculty, the teacher is likely to believe that the status quo is good, at least for his own department, and he is reluctant to see it changed.

IV

In this conservative atmosphere, the burden of proof is heavily on the proponents of change. In all probability they cannot *demonstrate* that their proposals will have the hoped-for beneficial results. They can gain supporters only by developing an intense commitment and personal dedication to their program. The essential degree of advocacy is difficult for faculty members, who are not zealots by nature or training. Colleagues are likely to respond more positively to understatement than to exaggeration, and they usually are suspicious of zealots and of utopias. Proponents of change thus face a troublesome dilemma. Unless they have real conviction and enthusiasm for their proposal, they are not able to gain necessary support; but if they are drawn into optimistic claims by the resistance of colleagues, their tactical position is weakened.

V

The faculty member has an artistic or public-service view of his profession. He did not become a teacher and scholar because he expected large economic rewards. For this reason, he is likely to be unimpressed by economic solutions to problems. Perhaps one reason for his choice was that the principles and competitive practices of business were distasteful to him. He does not believe that teaching can be analyzed as a business analyzes its activities. The concepts of "management," "productivity" and "utilization" applied to education are, in his judgment, inappropriate if not offensive. He is deeply troubled by the necessity of paying his family bills, but if his wife writes the checks she is likely to have a keener sense of the family's financial needs than he. In any event, his colleagues' financial situation and prospects are not remarkably better than his. By speaking of the "economic status of the profession" he can express his need for a higher income without personalizing it.

VI

A change in an educational program inevitably means a change in the habits of some members of the faculty. As we know from other situations, change can appear as a threat to the individuals involved. For the person who is psychologically insecure, the familiar is comforting and he has a deep-seated need to resist change. But change may be strongly resisted for other reasons. On casual examination, the kind of educational program implicit in the Models of the Possible can be disturbing in several possible ways. The individual who derives his greatest satisfaction from his professional prestige may see his career threatened because, if he has more students, or if he has to prepare new courses, there will be less time for the research on which he thinks his professional prestige rests. An individual accustomed to lecturing to small groups, or to the discussion method, may fear that he will be forced to use teaching methods which are strange or unsuited to him. If the number of courses are to be reduced, a teacher may have to give up a course in which he has deep interest; or he may be asked to give up an established course and prepare a new one. Or, if there are to be fewer teachers in proportion to the students, a teacher may be apprehensive about his job.

These reactions to change may or may not be articulated by an individual. But we know that human beings do react in these ways. There is no reason to believe that in this regard faculty members are different.

VII

Many teachers believe that the tutorial method is ideal from the standpoint of educational effectiveness. Next in order of preference is a group small enough to permit use of the Socratic method, with all students participating. Least desirable is thought to be the lecture course so large that the teacher cannot get to know his students. These views are held in spite of numerous studies showing that students taught in large classes perform on examinations about as well as students taught in small classes, and in spite of a centuries-long history of effective lecturing by talented teachers for appropriate subject matter. There is also, of course, the widely accepted but unproved belief that the lower the student-teacher ratio in an institution, the higher the quality of education.

A teacher with these attitudes is likely to conclude that any proposal to increase the average number of students per teacher necessarily implies a deterioration in educational quality. Consequently, he should oppose it on "educational grounds," irrespective of any other consideration.

VIII

Finally, a faculty member may not be willing to work for a more efficient educational program simply because he does not believe that the savings will benefit the faculty. Proposals for more effective use of teaching resources often lack concreteness about what is to be done with the savings. Faculty members tend to believe that there has been a proliferation of administrative staff disproportionate to the increase in the size of the faculty. A college usually needs new buildings. An "athletics-for-all" program is increasingly expensive. Under these circumstances, a faculty member may feel that savings in the instructional budget will be used for new building funds, to increase undergraduate scholarships, to meet the athletic deficit, to expand the alumni and public-relations offices or for other purposes peripheral to the main purpose of the institution. A faculty member also may believe that a reduction in the size of his department will simply make it possible for another and competing department to expand, or that the elimination of courses of interest to him will be offset by the introduction in other departments of new courses of interest to the President, Trustees or influential alumni. Here too there is a dilemma. Many faculty members would be deeply offended by the offer of a commitment that faculty salaries will be increased by the amount saved if the faculty accepts proposals for a change in educational program. But in the absence of such a commitment, the normal suspicion of academic bureaucracy operates.

Organizing for Change

The analysis thus far is intended to show the importance of organizational and motivational factors in "achieving the possible." If the analysis is valid, a college undertaking curricular reforms along the lines suggested by the models faces an extremely difficult task. No close observer of American institutions of higher education is likely to assume that the necessary action will follow readily once the need for it has been established. There are too many built-in resistors, too many plausible reasons for inaction, for so immediate and happy a result. But where to start?

I

For a particular institution, the first step is to determine whether it is facing a serious crisis. There are perhaps a few colleges so richly endowed, so well supported, that their concern is simply how their wealth may be used most advantageously. There are other private colleges whose existence at present is so precarious that they are on the verge of economic and educational collapse. Between these extremes are many institutions which are not in imminent danger but whose future may in fact be dubious. These institutions are a national resource which must be conserved if the American "mixed" system of public and private education is to continue. This Report may be especially useful for this group. How should action be initiated?

Assuming that this Report is distributed to faculty, Board of Trustees and administrative officers, the President might request the faculty to select by preferential ballot a group of representatives to confer with him and the Trustees. The assignment of the committee is to ask and answer several critical questions. The central question is simply this: Does it appear that this institution will be able to compete for high-quality faculty and students over the next 10 years, when competition for both will be increasingly severe? Or, stated differently, does the status quo, projected over the next 10 years, amount to a healthy institution, economically and educationally?

The first critical area is the faculty. Is the college now able to compete on favorable terms with state universities and strong private institutions for the most promising young teachers? Is it able to retain the experienced teachers it wishes to keep? If so, does the college have assured means of doubling its present salary scales in the next 10 years? If it is not now able to compete, or if the doubling of salaries does not appear to be feasible, there is cause for concern.

As to students: is the college now able to attract all of the qualified students it can accommodate? If not, is this situation of recent origin, or of some years' standing? What proportion of the student body is receiving scholarship aid? What proportion of scholarship expense is met from general funds? What proportion of a class graduates four years after entering college? How much of the attrition is caused by academic failure? Do the answers to these questions indicate that the institution's position is stable, improving or deteriorating?

Other questions have to do with plant and curriculum. Is the institution now of an economic size? There is of course no precise standard to apply, but the critical minimum size appears to be somewhere between 800 and 1,000 students. If the institution is significantly below this range and is not exceptionally wealthy, it should investigate the feasibility of larger enrollments. If the plant is not used for educational purposes during the summer, would the reorganization of the calendar and curriculum to include a summer session bring the enrollment for the year up to critical size? If an increase in enrollment would require additional plant, could the needed plant be financed without using funds otherwise available for salaries? Can the curriculum be arranged so that the additional enrollment could be handled without a proportionate increase in faculty?

The answer to this last question obviously requires close examination of the present curriculum and teaching methods. What is the average number of students per teacher? How many courses are offered each semester? What are the enrollments in these courses? What does an analysis of class size show? How many classes have fewer than 5 students? Between 5 and 10 students? And so on, up to the largest class? How many courses are required for graduation? How many hours does the student with a normal course load spend in the classroom each week? Are there significant differences among the departments? Are there special courses or programs which do not attract many students but which the college maintains because it has established a reputation in the field? Does the teaching load provide time for the teacher's professional growth and development? How many different courses does he teach during the year? How many hours does he spend in the classroom each week?

These questions are not exhaustive and are given here simply to illustrate the nature of the study which the committee should undertake. Comparable data from other institutions would be helpful. It is essential, of course, that all of the significant factors be projected for a considerable period. Only by this means can reasonably adequate conclusions be reached about the present state and the future of the college. If the committee concludes that the present program and future requirements cannot be supported by foreseeable resources, it should next consider how the institution can best be organized for the task of designing and administering a new program better fitted to its needs and resources.

II

This is the heart of the problem. A "mechanism" must be adopted which will command the support of faculty, administration and Board of Trustees when cherished prerogatives and deeply imbedded interests are questioned. Obviously, there can be no assured solution to this problem. Even the most promising solution for a particular institution is certain to encounter limitations and imperfections which can wreck the whole enterprise. Crises can be tolerated, endured and overcome if, and only if, there is a common dedication to the task and a continuing willingness to accept resourceful and energetic leadership. Lacking this essential motivation, no organizational arrangement can be successful.

Whatever form the "mechanism" may take, it is unlikely to be effective unless it meets certain criteria.

The "mechanism" must be suited to the traditions, personnel and current circumstances of the institution.

Centralized leadership is essential. A college is a diverse institution, and the typical curriculum is incredibly complex. Sound planning for change requires central direction and coordination of the various elements of the plan. Moreover, it is clear that the models of Part 3 cannot be achieved if planning is controlled by department-centered interests.

The "mechanism" must be capable of imaginative planning and of implementing its plans. At least four things are involved. First, it must understand the broad purpose and essential content of a liberal, as distinct from a vocational, education. Second, it must be informed about the nature of the crisis, in both its general and local aspects. Third, it must evoke imagination and initiative throughout the faculty. Fourth, it must be sensitive to faculty needs and attitudes and be able to win faculty support for extraordinary measures.

Finally, there must be in the "mechanism," and eventually throughout the college, a sharp sense of responsibility and accountability for the recommendations made and the actions taken.

Three different solutions to the problem of organizing for change are discussed in the following paragraphs. No doubt there are other possibilities which will emerge as a college begins to seek the best answer in its own situation. It is important to say that there is no one answer, and, indeed, the "mechanism" selected at the outset may be changed with experience. But whatever form is chosen, it is not likely to be successful unless it meets reasonably well the criteria enumerated above.

III

The President of the college obviously satisfies most of these criteria. He is part of the national leadership in educational matters and is its most natural source in his own institution. He presumably has the full confidence of the Board of Trustees, with whom he can share, without public discussion, the perplexities that are bound to arise. An individual can more easily provide energetic leadership and advocacy than can a group. A proposal acceptable to a group is likely to be weakened by compromise; and even if it is not, the members of the group will support it with varying degrees of conviction and enthusiasm. There are other advantages. The President has easy access to relevant information from his own and other institutions; and although he is separated from the faculty by their conception of his role, he can count upon the help of at least some faculty colleagues in the development and implementation of his ideas. No one is likely to have a keener sense of responsibility or be more directly accountable for the institution's welfare. Finally, in the history of American higher education there is evidence that leading institutions achieve eminence under strong presidential leadership. In all of these respects the presidency seems to be the "mechanism" for which we are looking.

In evaluating this possibility, it should be remembered that in the past 25 years or more the President's job has become more diverse and exacting. Even if he wishes to, the President cannot give up easily the public aspects of his job. These include the necessity of seeing to it that his institution is properly financed; and even though the program presented in the main parts of this report is in an important way a financial program, its benefits are not likely to be available for many years. Meanwhile, money will have to be raised from outside sources. The President is responsible for the institution in all of its aspects. This responsibility requires, for example, that he give of his time and energy to students, parents, alumni and Trustees, as well as to the faculty; and that he concern himself with extracurricular as well as curricular matters. A President can do all of these things and also be a prime source of educational leadership only if he is able to give educational policy whatever time and attention it requires.

A President may have certain handicaps as an educational leader, particularly in colleges of more than 1,000 students, simply because he is President. The instructional program is only one of the claimants for the institution's financial resources. The President and Board of Trustees annually must make decisions about how much is to be spent for instruction, how much for student scholarships, how much for plant maintenance and new construction, how much for administration, athletics and other extracurricular activities. Their decisions carry disappointment, some of which inevitably falls on the faculty. The accumulation of these disappointments over the years is likely to lessen the faculty's enthusiasm for the President, if not their confidence in him.

Equally important is the faculty's real attitude toward presidential leadership. On the one hand, the President's capacity for educational leadership is usually said to be a factor in his selection, and especially so if a faculty committee participates in the choice. But it is undoubtedly true, also, that many faculty members are more comfortable with an educational leader who is not too vigorous in his espousal of innovations.

A President who takes his educational-leadership function seriously encounters growing criticism and resentment as his policies begin to disturb the status quo. Eventually he must choose the course which his presidency is to follow. If he is sufficiently wise, forceful and persistent, he may be able to mold the institution to his vision, but at an ever-increasing price in terms of an equable personal and institutional life. If he lacks the personality and taste for this, he can try to exert his influence in inconspicuous and subtle ways. And if he is clever, persistent and has a reasonably long tenure, he may be able to accomplish by stratagem what he could not do directly. Or, recognizing the difficulties and beset by the demands of his several constituencies, he may choose to leave active educational leadership to others.

In spite of the difficulties, it is clear that the "mechanism" can and should be provided by the presidency under appropriate circumstances. But it may not be the best solution for some institutions, and the question remains of whether there may be some other way of organizing for change.

IV

A second obvious alternative is a faculty-centered "mechanism." There are advantages to this approach. Educational policy is traditionally the domain of the faculty. To turn away from the faculty completely in the present crisis would be to imply that neither the faculty as a body nor as individuals are capable of discharging a basic institutional responsibility. The effect upon morale could be disastrous. Moreover, each member of the faculty has given long years to preparing himself for teaching and writing, and he has committed his life to his subject and to education. Who is more dedicated than he to the cause, or more competent to serve it?

While all of this is true, it is not all of the truth. The continuing fragmentation of the curriculum by specialization and vocational interests—the cause of much of the present difficulty—occurred under faculty control of educational policy. In addition, structural defects in faculty organization—both a cause and an effect of specialization—are a major obstacle to the restoration of collective faculty responsibility for the formulation and administration of the curriculum.

Suppose, however, that the most competent and influential members of a college faculty recognized the urgency of the situation, and that they were associated formally for the task of leading and supporting a sustained effort to reorganize the institution's curriculum. *If* such a group had the encouragement and full support of the President and Board, and *if* it could command the continuing support of faculty colleagues, it would certainly be a hopeful and desirable solution to the problem of "achieving the possible."

V

A third alternative incorporates elements of the first two. Having recognized the importance of the subject and the urgency of action, the college might establish a "Council for Educational Policy and Program." This Council should have continuing responsibility for planning the curriculum required by the model which has been formally adopted and accepted by the Trustees.

The Council should not be concerned with the content of individual courses, except perhaps with lecture courses planned for a large segment of the student body. It must be concerned with the purpose and size of the institution, the total number of courses offered, the number of departmental courses, the ratio of teachers to students, the distribution of courses among the three main types outlined in the models, and the timing for effecting the plan eventually selected as best for the institution.

It is highly desirable that the charter of the Council be accepted in advance by the faculty, President and Trustees. For this reason, full discussion of the purposes of the Council prior to its establishment would be necessary. In most institutions it is likely that both the faculty and Board of Trustees will wish to retain the formal right of final approval of the Council's major recommendations. For practical purposes, this means that the Council is in essence a fact-finding and recommending body; but it should be agreed that its major recommendations will be accepted and not modified in essential respects, by faculty, President or Trustees.

The Council should be relatively small, with perhaps a maximum of 12 members. It should be constituted so that it will carry great prestige on the campus. In some institutions representatives of the Board may contribute to this result; in other institutions the reverse may be true. In most circumstances, the President or his representative should be chairman. But it is possible that in other situations the chairman should be a senior member of the faculty, or a member of the Board with a faculty member as co-chairman. The choice of the chairman is of critical importance, and it should be made only after the most careful analysis of particular needs and personnel resources of the institution. The principal qualifications for membership are: insight with respect to liberal education, the experience necessary to refine and evaluate this insight and the ability to implement plans and ideas. Although these qualifications are desirable for each member of the Council, they are especially important for the members selected from the administration and Board. Lacking them, these members cannot function as the equals of their faculty colleagues in the crucial areas of the Council's work.

The work of the Council will be time-consuming for every member. Certainly for the chairman and preferably for other members, the assignment should be considered a part of normal responsibilities and not simply added on to an otherwise full schedule. This arrangement will attest to the institution's conviction in the overriding priority of the Council's work, and it will also help assure the energy which the Council must have to do its job.

Obviously one of the Council's most basic tasks is to obtain a faculty consensus in support of its proposal. Opportunity for full discussion is essential, but it should be agreed when the Council is established that discussion in the faculty body will be concerned with the major principles, not the details, of the proposal and that discussion will not become an excuse for delay and indecision.

Before selecting this "mechanism," its weaknesses should be understood. If it is viewed as a compromise, attractive because of the weakness of the President or faculty, or because of faculty suspicion of the President, or as a device for neutralizing Trustee interest, it is clearly the least desirable of the possibilities. It would be better not to do anything than to form a Council for these reasons. There is also a serious question as to whether any council, however carefully chosen and however warmly welcomed at its inception, could survive the recurring crises which must be expected, during which responsibility for hard decisions would of necessity be assumed by the President and Trustees. Moreover, if it is to be effective, the Council will need strong leadership from both President and faculty. If the President is chairman of the Council, it is certain that some members of the faculty will feel that their colleagues on the Council were dominated by him. This problem would be aggravated if there were also Trustee members of the Council.

In short, the chief attraction of the Council as a "mechanism" is that it provides a way of bringing together the essential elements of the institution in a concerted effort. Its chief weakness is that it is by no means clear that adequate collective leadership can be sustained for the arduous tasks ahead.

VI

To summarize, once a college has made the initial decision to reorganize its curriculum to achieve the objectives outlined in this Report, its choice of a "mechanism" for the design and administration of the curriculum should be determined by its own traditions, needs, talents and genius for organization. Whatever the "mechanism," it is clear that a "model" can be achieved only by gradual steps taken over a period of a few or many years. During the transition period, it is essential that the institution watch carefully the progress of the successive steps for implementing its plan. Obvious tasks are periodic reporting on progress to faculty and Board of Trustees, and resourceful attention to ways and means of drawing into the effort all faculty members who can contribute to the solution of problems.

Unless there is continuous scrutiny of progress and periodically renewed determination to accomplish the planned change, initial enthusiasm and momentum will be lost in the difficulties and frustrations which are certain to occur. This is a critical consideration to be carefully weighed in the institution's choice of a "mechanism." Strong leadership, particularly in the administration of the teaching program and personnel policies, is essential to the survival of the plan. Can an ordinary committee serve this function? Probably not. Could a Council? Perhaps, under favorable circumstances. The presidency is the natural source of this leadership; and in many institutions, perhaps smaller ones particularly, the President can most easily serve this function. But whatever the size of the institution and whatever the "mechanism," the President and faculty must join in common cause if the planned change is to take place.

The most pervasive concern is to win the continuing consent of the three major elements—faculty, administration, and Trustees. Here the central problem is to develop within the college a concept of a public and institutional interest which is paramount to departmental and other special interests, and in accordance with which the curriculum will be designed and administered.

The creating of unity among diversity, the reconciling and, if necessary, the subordination of special interests to the general, has always been a democratic society's most challenging task. It is especially so in a pure democracy, and the liberal college is perhaps our closest approximation to a pure democracy.

There are many of these colleges in America, and no one

can predict where leadership will arise. The colleges which are now regarded as the strongest may not in fact be the source of this leadership. An institution under stress is likely to see its problems more clearly and be more resourceful and determined in seeking solutions than an institution confident of survival without extraordinary effort on its part. Complacency is often the twin of prestige.

PART 5

The Informed Trustee, a Major Responsibility of the President

Having considered Models of the Possible and the Achievement of the Possible, this Report now returns to the Trustee as the locus of final responsibility and authority and considers certain kinds of information which the Trustee needs to perform his function for the liberal college. Not every Board of Trustees includes sufficient members presently able to discharge adequately their responsibilities as Trustees of their college. When a Board of Trustees lacks this ability, it must be strengthened by the substitution or by the addition of persons qualified and willing to serve the college in a Trustee capacity.

An informed Trustee will serve his trusteeship better than a Trustee who assumes his position simply as a matter of honorific or social status. To be sure, a little knowledge is a dangerous thing, and no Trustee can possibly be informed on all matters affecting the welfare of his college. Still, as applied in general to all Trustees of all liberal colleges, relevant information as a preliminary to decision making would generally be accepted as a sound policy, even though difficult to achieve.

Since no Trustee can possibly be completely informed, the information which he does receive will be at least that which a tradition of periodic reports has established as appropriate, plus additional statistics and documentation affecting current issues that may be before the Board for decision or advice. The individual Trustee's own requests for information are frequently developed in a form suitable for Board presentation.

But there are so many facts, so much to know, and so little time! True; and just for this reason, the business of informing the Trustee is an important technical problem for the liberal college. Yet it is neglected and pushed aside. The routine of conventional schedules makes it certain that certain "facts will have been before them." But a basketful of facts will not make an informed Trustee, any more than it will make an informed administrative officer.

The existence of standing committees helps in dividing the work of Trustees, but the standing committee can be improperly used to conceal as well as to inform. The ad-hoc Special Committee is likely to serve a useful purpose if the members will cooperate and not leave the chairman with an issue too hot to handle in an open Board meeting.

Public Relations

The most compelling single area in which a Trustee needs to be informed is that vast and sprawling morass called "public relations." Only the most naive, uninformed or cynical will argue that the reason for the deep importance of public relations for a liberal college is that it is the basis for money raising. And yet, because of the present financial poverty and anxiety of most liberal colleges, the presentation of a chosen face to the public is today usually deliberately motivated by the hope of cash receipts to the treasury sooner or later. This distortion is caused by real and present need, but it weakens the usefulness of the liberal college in its service of liberal education.

In order to make an intelligent public-relations contribution, a Trustee must be informed as to the educational policies of his college. He needs to understand the educational and noneducational issues that are in dispute, as between faculty, administration, students, secondary schools, alumni, local community, other public or private institutions of higher learning, segments of the press, or even doubts that the President of the college himself may have as to whether all is as it should be.

The Trustee so informed can be expected to make his appropriate and affirmative contribution to the evolving educational personality of his college, whether in discussions within the meetings of the Trustee cabinet, in personal and familiar circles, in his community, in his trade association, or with Trustees and administrators of other educational institutions.

Financial and Operational Data

After public-relations sophistication, the college Trustee next needs (1) financial and (2) operational information, first for prudence in helping make the decisions that are the responsibility of the Trustees and second for justice in evaluating the skill and courage of the administrative officers.

INFORMATION ON FINANCE

The financial information which a Trustee needs falls into three separate classifications. The first is "balance-sheet" data, the second is "budgetary," and the third is "financial projections" for shorter or longer periods ahead.

A. THE BALANCE SHEET.   The balance sheet discloses the assets and liabilities of the college as of a moment of time, stated as best they can be as dollar values. This is the statement of the property of the college, the material substance at its disposal to get its job done.

The balance-sheet information can be almost unlimited in scope and in detail. Unless it is skillfully organized and presented, the end result will be confusion and frustration rather than awareness of a starting point from which a new beginning can always be made. There is likely to be at least one Trustee who has a jigsaw-puzzle motivation in the presence of a balance sheet; he delights in bringing order out of chaos; he will be the great friend of the President, the Treasurer, or financial officer under whatever name. And he can make it possible for the other Trustees to use their best wisdom and common sense in the handling of the property of the college.

The basic problem in making balance-sheet data meaningful is proper classification and consolidation, and this, well done, is always done with the operational decisions of the college in mind. The large college, or even the medium-sized institution today, has a varied set of duties and responsibilities which are carried out in transactions that leave a financial residue. These must all be finally associated in the balance sheet of the college as of the close of its fiscal year.

Each college will have its own ideas and traditions as to how the items in this schedule of property should be divided. However, we can be reasonably sure that the following classifications can be found.

1. Income-producing assets such as endowments not used in the operation of the college, stocks, bonds, etc.

2. Income-producing assets used in the operation of the college, dormitories, etc.

3. Assets used in the operation of the college but not directly income-producing, such as academic buildings and grounds.

4. Assets held by the college for an indefinite future, neither used nor income-producing, such as real estate held for future uses.

5. Properties held under management arrangements.

Liabilities are of the conventional kind, but by and large they will be associated with the purpose for which they were incurred. For example, if funds have been borrowed to build dormitories, this debt should be associated with the dormitory account; if they have been borrowed to provide adequate year-end balances, they will be associated with the capital funds. The ordinary college will have no general liabilities other than a small residue of bills payable at the end of its fiscal year—and in a well-run institution that has any credit at all, there will always be some of these.

But except for the financially-minded Trustee, most of this information, essential though it is, makes little difference in his Trustee behavior or in the educational policies of the college. There are certain points, however, that all Trustees should have an opinion about. These include:

1. To what extent is the investment portfolio directed to future capital gains rather than current income? This question raises a point that the Finance Committee is hardly qualified to decide; namely, are the resources of the college to be used for the present generation of students and faculty or for some future group which will be in college when the deferred present income materializes? Are realized capital gains expendable, and if so, to what extent and for what purposes? Finance Committees and finance officers have a natural appetite for low income now, but with constant appreciation in the asset value of the portfolio. For a tax-paying individual or institution, this is understandable, and for some colleges it may be good public-relations policy, but it is clearly an issue for a Board of informed Trustees to decide.

2. In the second place the Trustees should be informed as to the nature of limitations, if any, on the use of the capital that is listed as "capital funds" or "endowment." This information is important, since it may be that considerable sums that appear to be restricted in fact are not restricted. Particular attention needs to be paid to various reserves and capital gains added to principal which have been set up in times past and now may have been lost under a symbol in the endowment account. Depreciation reserves on dormitories have a way of being swallowed up.

The reason for a clear understanding of funds available for college use is that an expansion program of a financially practical nature may be held back because the Trustees do not know that there are reserves or other capital funds freely at their disposal.

Other problems associated with the balance sheet are generally better left to the Executive and Finance Committees of the college. Many institutions will have special asset problems that should have informed Trustee consideration, but these are generally ad hoc situations and the proper committee will bring them to the Board of Trustees at the proper time.

B. THE BUDGET.   The budgetary statements of the college include last year's income and expenditures, this year's and next year's budget. The budget is a document potentially even more confusing than the balance sheet, and it is almost necessary for a college to have a designated Budget Committee to go over the details and bring back to the Board information and questions of general college interest.

It is in the budget that policy and program are expressed, and it is only by rigid self-discipline that the Budget Committee can avoid becoming a Policy Committee, in fact if not in name. For some colleges, this may be what the Board of Trustees wishes, but it is probably not good for the long-term health of the college.

There are several general questions that a Trustee needs to know about a budget:

1. Are the estimates of income realistic? Are any items substantially understated, such as income on endowment or current gifts from alumni or tuition income?

2. What reserves are being set up? Are they adding excessively to reserves already in existence?

3. What discretionary items are on the expenditure side? Who has control? Were the final results reported for last year?

4. If a deficit is projected, how will it be financed? How would a larger one be handled? What has the record been?

5. If a surplus is shown, what purpose will be made of

this year's surplus in the next year's budget? Or, do the Trustees approve the budgeting of an annual surplus as college policy? What has been the record on surpluses?

6. To what extent have funds available for general college use been allocated for scholarships or other student aid? What is the policy?

7. What is the financial picture on noncurricular activities? What are the prospects for next year?

8. What is the pricing policy on noncurricular activities? Are the dormitories and dining halls being run at a loss? What about student and alumni events? Publications? There is nothing sinister about taking such losses provided the operations are efficiently managed and the pricing policy consciously adopted is responsible for the deficiency. In many cases, such losses are unknown, though traditional, and serve no useful purpose.

9. The administrative budget is primarily the responsibility of the Executive Committee. But the Trustee should be informed as to what percentage and how much of tuition receipts are going for administration, and how much are going for noncurricular student activities.

C. FINANCIAL PROJECTIONS. The liberal college is in a period of economic and financial change. These changes are primarily due to conditions over which the college has no control. But this does not mean that the college cannot mold the future into a pattern something more according to its wish than otherwise might come to be. It can detect inconsistencies in the projection of its present fiscal behavior. It can erect barriers against sweeping tendencies that would irreparably alter its character and personality. It can avoid commitments that do not recognize implacable necessity. For all these reasons, the liberal college today requires a projection of its economic and financial future.

But this arithmetical projection of the future will be almost meaningless without some definite policy determination on essential matters of curriculum and methods of instruction. Here the future is obscure except in one respect. The future of the curriculum and of teaching methods cannot be a projection of the past. It cannot be a projection of the past because there isn't enough money in hand or potentially available to pay the salaries that will be required for a faculty of any kind, to say nothing of a good one, to continue today's type of college. There aren't enough alumni or other gifts either for current expense or for endowment. Tuitions cannot be sufficiently raised even on the plea that there's no debt so satisfactory as a debt for a college degree, if not for a liberal education. Federal or other public assistance to the private liberal college in adequate amounts is an idle dream. Increasing the number of students is no solution, unless the student-teacher ratio is raised. Better use of plant will help if an enlarged student body becomes available. We know that there will be more students ready to go to college, but what about *this* particular college for whose future *this* particular Trustee is partially but specifically responsible?

All these questions will be raised, the uncertain future scene will be opened up, if financial projections for at least five years ahead are placed before the Board.

The informed Trustee is entitled to have the basic facts of administrative and educational programming before him while there are still opportunities for the consideration of alternatives. These basic facts include projections of student enrollment, faculty salaries, ratio of teachers to students, contemplated changes in tuition or dormitory rentals, new buildings or building alterations required, general plans to mobilize alumni or public support.

These financial and educational projections are becoming an urgent necessity for all liberal colleges. They are becoming urgent because of the imminent and drastic upward pressure on academic salaries.

INFORMATION ON OPERATIONS

Two general types of operational information exist; the first deals with the curriculum or teaching program, the second deals with everything else. By and large the latter, the extracurricular operating information, pertains to matters which are best observed by special committees of the Board with special interests or which are delegated by the Board to operating officers or to committees of alumni that are happy to take over the detailed responsibility for overseeing specific activities.

The care of buildings and grounds requires the supervision of a special Trustee committee, since either under- or overmaintenance can result in final operational budget figures of a most misleading character.

Two other extracurricular activities of great importance to the college are (1) dormitories and student housing, including provisions made by the college for student meals, and (2) student activities, including athletics.

Good housing and proper nourishment are a necessary part of a college educational program. This is true even of a nonresidential college, where perhaps little can be done about it. However, the problems are so detailed and so technical that the Trustees must depend on special interests either within or outside the Board for proper supervision. Information as to results, however, should be available, even though it is not included on the agenda of regular Trustee meetings.

Student extracurricular activities including athletics have important over-all educational values and must be considered part of, and administered along with, the educational program as a whole. These activities may have large financial implications, both for building and for expense, and they may have a public-relations importance that carries them beyond any educational purpose relevant to the specific individuals involved in the activity. The Trustees as a whole must take final

responsibility for the wholesomeness and relative financial
burden of the students' extracurricular activities, and they
must be informed so that they can meet this responsibility in
good conscience. There is, of course, no objection to alumni
participation in overseeing these activities, provided only that
alumni and Trustees see pretty much eye-to-eye on basic policy and relative emphasis. The purpose of the intercollegiate
athletic program may be to raise money and to get publicity.
If so, so be it. But the responsibility is the Trustees' and they
must be organized to be informed as to what their agents are
doing in their behalf in this somewhat dynamic area.

Curriculum and Methods of Instruction

Turning now to the informational requirements of Trustees in the most difficult area of all, the curriculum and methods of instruction, we cannot generalize, except negatively at
one point: the Trustees of the true liberal college wish to preserve academic freedom and accordingly they are not interested and do not wish to be informed as to what transpires in
the particular classroom between the teacher and his students.

This is a funny kind of business! The specific persons responsible, the Trustees, cannot supervise—manage, if you
please—what is the essence of the business: the educational
process itself where it goes on, in classroom or lecture hall.
And yet that is the heart of this particular kind of business.
There must be freedom of inquiry, and freedom of instruction
for the teacher and for the student. And forever and forever
more, once the teacher is granted academic tenure by the
Trustees.

The basis of this extraordinary situation, academic freedom of expression backed up by academic tenure, lies in two
beliefs: first, that the individual who has been granted academic freedom will use his privileges according to what might
be called an academic conscience, that is, he will not teach his

students as true what he himself knows to be false; second, that if the teacher should in good conscience be in error, free discussion in the classroom, on the campus, in another class, reading and general free communication will bring victory to the truth. In contrast, consider the opposite policy; supervising and authenticating all the teaching and writing of the members of a faculty! It has been tried, but it is not the way of the American liberal college.

The acceptance of the principles of academic freedom and academic tenure is so widespread in this country that the subject gets little public attention and on most campuses is rarely debated. Recently, much excitement has been caused by the issue of Communist affiliation, but this is really an issue that pertains to the existence of the academic conscience and the nature of truth rather than a questioning of the principle of academic freedom itself.

The critical point, however, is that the reality of academic freedom and academic tenure belongs to the individual member of the faculty as an essential ingredient of his teaching and his scholarly activity. Freedom and tenure are recognition of his personal conscience and personal integrity while he is engaged in his personal activity of working with students and with his subject matter. These freedoms are freedoms of the individual; the individual holds them against difference of opinion, and he is sustained and protected in holding and exercising them by all the administrative structure and Trustee powers of the college that have made its commitment to him and through him to liberal education.

Academic freedom and academic tenure are precious privileges in today's world of violence, disorder, lust for power, fear and cynicism with respect to values of every kind. Both the giving and the receiving of these privileges are taken too much for granted in our colleges and universities. They have been wrongly used by academic institutions as a substitute for adequate compensation, and they have been accepted, not because they give assurance for self-confidence in intellectual adventure, but because they give employment and salary security. The individual with academic tenure is freed from the rat-race for employment and status, and this is as it should be. But neither the individual nor the institution granting these privileges should defile them by throwing them into the scales along with the financial substance of academic employment.

The privileges of academic freedom and academic tenure, being, as they are, directly associated with an individual's conscience, his awareness of right and wrong, his sense of duty, cannot be transferred by him to another; nor can they be appropriated by a group of which he and others like him are members. A group of individuals do not have as a group the individual's essential person from which his rights are derived and to which his privileges adhere. The faculty of a college, the departments of that faculty, the subsections organized for whatever purpose of convenience or necessity, do not as such partake of the spiritual quality of the individual person which gives the warrant for his rights and privileges. The faculty of a college in the aggregate does not have academic freedom, the departments of a faculty do not have academic tenure. There is no reason why the administration of a college or why the Trustees of a college should not be informed on all matters of faculty or departmental jurisdiction and management, nor why they should not intervene in situations where the academic machinery is proving inadequate to its task.

Accordingly, the information required by the informed Trustee on matters of curriculum and methods of instruction does not infringe on any matters of academic privilege. The faculty as a body derives its jurisdiction from the Trustees; it is an agent for performing part of the work of the college. The faculty is not a repository for the rights and privileges of the individual members. These rights and privileges cannot be eliminated or collectivized; they would exist whether there was a body called the "faculty" or not.

The faculty has been the instrument for organizing the curriculum. It has depended on departmental initiative for substantive proposals, and on balance of power for its decisions. Under this system, the liberal college has deteriorated, its economic and financial position has become untenable. It cannot draw to its faculty the outstanding talent of its generation, although it still holds the prestige embodied in the ideal of "liberal education as preparation for the good life."

The Trustees must be informed as to what the faculty's administration of curriculum and methods of instruction has done to the liberal college. The Trustees must set some informed standards of performance on which their administrative officers can rely. The Trustees, to be successful, must accomplish these purposes with the cooperation of all, and above all must preserve for the individual faculty member the personal rights and privileges that are essential to the character of the liberal college.

Students, Teachers and the Curriculum

Certain statistical and financial information is clearly necessary to the informed Trustee. He needs to know by statistical summary what the members of the faculty are paid, what load they are under obligation to carry in classroom teaching, the extent to which this obligation is enforced, and when it is excused, how the difference is balanced.

With respect to the student body, the Trustees should be informed as to how many students are in each yearly class, how many were admitted to upper-class status, the relation of freshman admissions to freshman registrations, the relation of freshman applications to freshman admissions. The Trustees may also want facts on geographical distribution of students, applications and admissions as well as tendencies of concentration from particular secondary schools. It is likely that the years immediately ahead will bring problems of student num-

bers and student constituency that will require Trustee decision or at least Trustee guidance. Now is the time for testing
out the schedules and preparing the background statistical data
that will be the basis for decisions later on.

The Trustee should know the over-all figure on the ratio
of students to full-time teaching faculty in residence. This information is crucial in determining what can be done about
faculty compensation. Opinions will differ, but the Trustees
can examine models of distribution of students, courses and
faculty and, after consultation with the appropriate academic
agencies, come to a conclusion as to what model will best suit
their ideal for their particular college. From this model, many
operational, architectural and financial consequences will flow.
Any drift to insolvency can be stopped, even though years
may be required to attain an accepted model position.

The Trustees, in establishing general statistical standards
of prudent economic and financial management, need say
nothing specific about the content or method of any particular course. But because every course affects every other course
in the sense that all must fit into a harmonious pattern, certain
general indicators are required:

1. Ratio of students to full-time teaching faculty.

2. Average number of courses taught on a full-time basis
per faculty member.

3. Number of courses and sections offered per year.

4. Number of courses and sections designed to serve 10
or fewer students. This information is needed to implement
whatever policy on small-group instruction seems correct for
the particular liberal college.

5. Amount in dollars per student going to faculty compensation. With this figure in hand, a percentage relationship
can be established to total tuition or to any other fixed standard. The tendency for this figure to shrink percentagewise is
the indicator to be watched.

6. A model showing course and student distribution, similar to those developed in Part 3.

Information about enrollments in the numerous individual courses should be maintained routinely, but should not be provided Trustees except on special request. This data is so voluminous and is subject to such a variety of standards and explanations that no Trustee contribution is likely to justify making the material available and hearing it discussed. However, the Trustees should make sure that these breakdowns are in the hands of the administrative officers, and, for their own departments, of the department heads.

There are no doubt many other statistical and financial indicators of operational adequacy, but here only a minimum is proposed. If interpreted in their interrelationships, they will give the Trustee a firm sense of knowing what is going on, and by use of comparative figures, what the direction is and also, if and when the figures become available, how one college is doing in comparison with others.

The economic and financial material relating to the curriculum does not by any means exhaust the responsibilities of the Trustees with respect to the curriculum. Once the barrier is down between curriculum and Trustees, there are a number of issues, both current and emerging, that the Trustees may well take an interest in, possibly a decisive interest. One current problem of the curriculum is what to do about so-called remedial courses, those courses that are offered to make up for inadequacies in secondary-school preparation. For the most part, these are in English, mathematics and foreign languages. The liberal college will shortly, in all probability, be able to refuse admission to these poorly prepared students. But there is testimony that these students in many cases have marked intrinsic ability or unusual special talents! Is there not some way that the college can organize to see that the inadequacies are removed?

Then there is the question as to what the liberal college should do about its science offerings. Should it attempt to give professional work in science, or should it confine its program to the liberal science exposure that is needed by the educated citizen whatever his role in adult life? If so, what should be done for the student with authentic scientific talent who emerges from the ranks of the undergraduate student body?

Another pressing question for the liberal college is what to do about its offerings in modern languages. All agree that the ideal that has placed and kept the modern languages in the liberal-arts curriculum is valid. But can it be attained practically under present conditions of secondary-school preparation? Surely at the college level more should be expected than simple ability to read and converse in a language other than one's own. Desirable as this is of itself, the question of emphasis comes in, and this is not a question that a faculty body as a whole can fairly determine. Can the liberal college provide extracurricular facilities that will make possible basic linguistic preparation, so that courses in foreign literature and cultures can be offered that will meet justifiable collegiate standards of merit?

Finally, the Trustees should be currently informed of work in progress, tentative conclusions, and recommendations and decisions of such a Council for Educational Policy and Program as is recommended in Part 4, or of whatever mechanism may be set up. The contact between the members of the Council and members of the faculty will be continuous and spontaneous. The Trustees should also have preliminary indications of what the Council is thinking, so that they will not be confronted by recommendations for which they are completely unprepared.

The Informed Trustee

The informed Trustee need not be a nuisance. He should not be a gossip, nor be interested in anecdotal incidents having no significance as clinical clues to the quality of the college's operation. Above all, the informed Trustee must not consider himself a part-time administrative officer with a part-time program for which he has assumed a part-time personal interest. If the Trustee is chairman of a Board committee, he does have a special responsibility for the development of policy in the area of his committee. If he is out of sympathy with college policy in that particular area, he should stand aside. There is plenty of work for Trustees in their capacity as Trustees; we need not be worried about the harm that a minimum of relevant information will do them.

It may appear that the requirements for information herein set forth are excessive, that no college can expect its Trustees to take the time necessary to expose themselves to the data and schedules necessary for sound Trustee judgment.

However, properly organized, the material is not unduly burdensome. Some of the data merely support general schedules and can be ignored by all but those most concerned. Material should be sent to the Board in advance of the meeting at which it will be discussed, and if the administration wants action, the appropriate resolutions should be drawn and sent with the supporting data.

A Trustee cannot perform his function merely by attending meetings and filling in on his informational requirements by glancing at papers that have been placed before his seat. Nor can he be expected to be brought up to date informally by the President before and after the several sessions of the Board.

The responsibilities of the Trustees of our liberal colleges are both extensive and important. They are neither ambiguous nor self-defined. They are created by college charters, and each Trustee assumes his powers and responsibilities formally by accepting his election.

The colleges are part of the shadow government of the United States; they have status, duties and freedom. They have responsibilities for an immense area of liberal education, and we depend on liberal education to guide free men in the formation of their own consciences. The Trustees of the liberal colleges are participating in an historic period on a strategic front. Let them be informed, so that they can discharge their responsibilities with courage and with wisdom.